# MOURNING CHILD GRIEF SUPPORT GROUP CURRICULUM: PRESCHOOL EDITION

# MOURNING CHILD GRIEF SUPPORT GROUP CURRICULUM:

## Preschool Edition

## Denny the Duck Stories

Linda Lehmann, M.A., L.P.
Shane R. Jimerson, Ph.D.
Ann Gaasch, M.A.

BRUNNER-ROUTLEDGE
ALERE FLAMMAM
Taylor & Francis Group

| USA | Publishing Office: | BRUNNER-ROUTLEDGE |
| | | *A member of the Taylor & Francis Group* |
| | | 325 Chestnut Street |
| | | Philadelphia, PA 19106 |
| | | Tel: (215) 625-8900 |
| | | Fax: (215) 625-2940 |
| | Distribution Center: | BRUNNER-ROUTLEDGE |
| | | *A member of the Taylor & Francis Group* |
| | | 7625 Empire Drive |
| | | Florence, KY 41042 |
| | | Tel: 1-800-634-7064 |
| | | Fax: 1-800-248-4724 |
| UK | | BRUNNER-ROUTLEDGE |
| | | *A member of the Taylor & Francis Group* |
| | | 27 Church Road |
| | | Hove |
| | | E. Sussex, BN3 2FA |
| | | Tel.: +44 (0) 1273 207411 |
| | | Fax: +44 (0) 1273 205612 |

**MOURNING CHILD GRIEF SUPPORT GROUP CURRICULUM: PRESCHOOL EDITION: Denny the Duck Stories**

1 2 3 4 5 6 7 8 9 0

Printed by G. H. Buchanan, Philadelphia, PA, 2000.
Cover design by Rob Williams.

A CIP catalog record for this book is available from the British Library.
  The paper in this publication meets the requirements of the ANSI Standard Z39.48-1984 (Permanence of Paper).

Library of Congress Cataloging-in-Publication Data
Lehmann, Linda.
    Mourning child grief support group curriculum : preschool  edition : Denny the duck stories /
  Linda Lehmann, Shane R. Jimerson, Ann Gaasch.
      p. cm.
    Includes bibliographical references and index.
    ISBN 1-58391-097-2 (pbk. : alk. paper)
    1. Grief in children—Study and teaching. 2. Bereavement in children—Study and teaching.
  3. Children and death—Study and teaching. 4. Loss (Psychology) in children—Study and
  teaching. 5. Children—Counseling of—Study and teaching. I. Jimerson, Shane R.
  II. Gaasch, Ann.  III. Title.

BF723.G75 L46 2000
155.9'37'0833—dc21

                                                                                    00-064663

ISBN 1-58391-097-2 (paper)

# Contents

# Preface

The Mourning Child Preschool grief support curriculum is intended for use with preschool children who have experienced the death of someone special to them. It was designed for use by professionals who work in schools, hospitals, hospices, mental health agencies, or any setting that serves bereaved children. The curriculum contains lesson plans for 10 sessions that include age-appropriate activities that enable young children to approach highly sensitive and painful topics through a variety of fun and engaging activities. The user is guided through the curriculum with detailed instructions and learning objectives for each session. The curriculum encourages children who may have limited language to work through their feelings through play.

The curriculum is divided by age level so that the group activities are developmentally appropriate. This design also affords the participants an opportunity to meet peers that have had a similar loss. The activities have been designed to help youth approach their grief through a variety of engaging activities that allow for the expression of their grief. The variety of activities include drawing, sculpting, music, games, journaling, problem-solving, drama, stories, and movement, which are used throughout the curriculum to give youths an opportunity to express their grief. Participants are taught various tools that will help them cope with their grief even after the group ends. The Tasks of Grief form the path toward their healing and offer practical steps for them to take. The curriculum also provides structure participating youth can count on every session: the topics of the sessions change, the activities vary, but the format remains the same. The group sessions are intended to present youths with topics that alternate between "head work" and "heart work." Sessions that employ activities that tap into "head work" are intended to teach group members death education, coping, and self-care techniques. Sessions that tap into "heart work" are designed to help the youth get in touch with their feelings and the pain of their loss. The intent is to help them to learn about death and to explore their grief in order to understand both. It is recognized that there is no single appropriate grief sequence or experience; rather, the aim of this grief support group curriculum is to facilitate healthy variations of mourning and positive adaptations following the death of a close or special person.

# Introduction

## Grief is a Family Process

Children grieve within the context of the family. Loss impacts the entire family system. As part of this system, children learn about grief through observing, listening, and talking to their family members following an early loss. Ideally, a caregiver within the child's family will participate in an adult support group. Often groups are organized such that the caregivers attend a separate group during the same time that the children are participating in a group. The participation of the adults is important for several reasons.

First, it is likely that the adults will be experiencing their own grief responses, and participation in the group will facilitate healthy coping. Second, through participation in the support group, these caregivers will learn about individual differences in grief reactions; in other words, even within a family, individuals can have varied grief responses. Third, these adults will better understand information communicated in the children's groups and be more prepared to provide support for their children.

For instance, it is important that children understand that it is okay to be sad, mad, happy, and scared, and that it is okay to talk about these feelings. If the family does not talk about the death, share feelings, or grieve in a healthy way, it is not likely that children will. Furthermore, grief does not simply go away after a specific amount of time; it is normal for feelings to emerge years after the loss. Thus, it is important that caregivers who will be with the child years after the support group ends are informed about the way children mourn.

For these reasons we encourage those coordinating grief support groups for children to also orchestrate grief support groups for adults. These curricula are designed to address key components of grief in an age-appropriate manner in an effort to facilitate healthy mourning.

1

## ■ A Note to Group Facilitators

The grief support group is designed to provide support, not therapy. Some children may need to receive individual or family counseling instead of or in addition to the bereavement group. While there are a range of grief responses children may experience, it is important to take note of children who are experiencing strong responses (either in intensity or duration) and refer them for additional services. Support group facilitators are encouraged to attend to behaviors or communications that often indicate the need for a referral for individual therapeutic intervention, including: if a child gives the slightest hint of being at risk for suicide; if the child experiences sustained denial and refuses to acknowledge the death; if the child reports many headaches, stomachaches, etc. (e.g., psychosomatic problems); if the child is experiencing persistent sleep disorders such as nightmares, bed-wetting, etc.; if there is a prolonged period during which a child is unable to focus and concentrate on schoolwork, or daydreams frequently, and is unable to complete assignments; if there are severe changes in eating patterns—binge eating, not eating, etc.; if the child acts like the deceased person in order to bring him or her back or to gain favor with surviving family members; if the child displays prolonged regression to an earlier developmental level; and/or if the child fears the illness or experiences the symptoms of the deceased. The basic idea is to be sensitive to possible maladaptive manifestations of natural grief reactions and to provide appropriate referrals to meet the needs of each child. Any of the common grief reactions may be unhealthy if they persist or the child becomes consumed with a particular response. Thus, it is important to attend to both the intensity and duration of individual grief responses.

Please note that each item listed in the Materials Section of each week's curriculum is described fully in Appendix 1.

### ■ INTERVIEW SAMPLE
### Basic Information

## Instructions for Interviewer

Introduce self and explain position in agency. Ask if now would be a good time to talk or if it would be better to set up a different time. Explain that some information is needed to register the children for the group. Complete this form. Then fill out the full interview form, one for each child.

Name of primary caregiver: _____

Address: _____

Phone number: (Home) _____ (Work) _____

(Other) _____ Okay to leave a message? Yes _____ No _____

| Names of children | Gender | Birthdate | Grade |
|---|---|---|---|
| _____ | _____ | _____ | _____ |
| _____ | _____ | _____ | _____ |
| _____ | _____ | _____ | _____ |
| _____ | _____ | _____ | _____ |

How were you referred to our program?

_____

Name of deceased _____ Relationship _____

Cause of death _____ Date of death _____

## ■ Full Interview Sample

### Instructions for Interviewer

Fill out one form for each child to be enrolled in the program. Explain to callers that they do not need to answer these questions if they don't feel comfortable, but it is very helpful if something can be learned about the child before he or she starts the group. Explain that this information is confidential and will be shared only with the group facilitators. However, if physical or sexual abuse of a child is reported or if it is thought that they are going to hurt themselves or someone else confidentiality will be broken and the appropriate agency will be notified. Ask if they have any questions.

Child's name: _____

Interview date: _____    Group: _____

### School

Has your child ever been in a group before (include sports activities, daycare, clubs)? Describe.

_____

_____

### Reaction to Loss

Can you tell me a little bit more about your child's relationship with the deceased?

_____

_____

What feelings have you observed in your child since the death (sadness, anger, fear, happiness)? How do you know what your child is feeling (by behavior, by what they say)? What feelings do you think your child might not be expressing?

_____

_____

_____

_____

What are your concerns about your child? Why are you looking for a group now?

_____

_____

_____

_____

## Relationships

Do you identify with any specific religious affiliation? How was the death explained in terms of religious affiliation?

*Note*: if interviewees are strongly religious, inform them of the group's philosophy concerning spirituality and religion.

_____

_____

_____

## Health

Do you have any concerns about:

Physical Abuse _____

Sexual Abuse _____

Has your child ever:

been treated for depression _____

had thoughts about or tried to hurt him- or herself _____

had thoughts about or tried to hurt others _____

Is your child seeing a counselor? Who? Would you sign a release in case the group leaders should need or want to contact the counselor?

_____

_____

_____

# Grief Support Group Curriculum

## ■ Week 1: Information Interviews

### Materials

Grief Support Groups General Information Sheet (GIS)
(See below and Appendix 2 for GIS)

Children need a transition into the group experience. For this reason, the first session is an information interview. Facilitators meet with the children and their caregivers (parents or guardians) for a 20-minute interview. This appointment allows the family to find their way to the location of the groups, meet their facilitators, see the space in which their groups will meet, and talk to the facilitators about the program. Having the information interview prior to their entering the group helps to lessen their fears about the group experience, and get many of their questions about the group answered. The session also allows the group facilitators to meet the children and spend a little time getting to know them one-on-one.

It is important for the facilitators to gather information about the child's developmental history and grief experiences; therefore the GIS should be asked in a semistructured interview format with caregivers and the child present. A GIS should be filled out for each child. An additional copy of the GIS, for photocopies, is included in Appendix 2. After this initial session, the child is then ready to begin the group.

### Grief Support Groups General Information Sheet (GIS)

Child's name: _____

Today's date: _____ Date that the loss occurred: _____

First time participant in group? Yes _____ No _____

If no, how many times has your child participated in a group

prior to the current group? _____

## Who died?

Mother _____ Father _____ Sibling _____ Friend _____

Relative (specify) _____ Other (specify) _____

## How close was the child to the person that died?

Not at all close _____ Somewhat close _____ Close _____ Pretty close _____

Very close _____

## What was the cause of the death?

Illness _____ Accident _____ Sudden death (e.g., heart attack) _____

Suicide _____ Homicide ___

## Did the child witness the death?

Yes _____ No _____

## With whom does the child currently live?

Parent _____ (specify) Mother _____ Father _____ Sibling _____

Friend _____ Relative (specify) _____ Other (specify) _____

## Who provides the child's primary emotional support? (All that apply)

Parent _____ Sibling _____ Friend _____ Relative (specify) _____

Mental health practitioner (specify) _____

Religious representative (e.g., nun, pastor, rabbi, priest) _____

Other (specify) _____

## What other losses has the child experienced in his or her lifetime? (All that apply)

Death of a parent (specify) _____ Date of loss _____

Death of sibling (specify age of sibling) _____ Date of loss _____

Death of friend (specify) _____ Date of loss _____

Death of relative (specify) _____ Date of loss _____

Death of other significant person (specify) _____ Date of loss _____

Loss of home (specify) _____ Date of loss _____

Separation from sibling(s) (specify) _____ Date of loss _____

Loss of biological family unit: Foster care _____ or Adoption _____

Date of loss _____

## Had the child experienced any of the following prior to the loss? (All that apply)

Physical abuse _____ When _____Relationship to perpetrator _____

Sexual abuse _____ When _____ Relationship to perpetrator _____

Depression _____ When _____

Suicide attempt (s) _____ When _____

Addiction/substance abuse _____ When _____

## School

Does your child receive any special assistance at school such as tutoring, advanced placement, or special classes? (specify)

_____

_____

_____

Has the school environment been supportive of your child or have there been problems since the death? (provide details)

_____

_____

_____

## Reaction to Loss

How does your child most easily express him- or herself (talking, writing, art, physical games)?

_____

_____

_____

What would you like the group facilitator to know about your child?

_____

_____

_____

## Relationships

How would you describe your relationship with your child? How does your child relate to other family members?

_____

_____

_____

How would you describe your child's relationship with peers (ages of peers, extrovert, introvert, leader, follower)?

_____

_____

_____

## Health

Does your child have any health concerns? Any allergies? Has he or she had any serious injuries or illnesses? Is your child taking any medications?

_____

What is your child's most frequent health problem?

_____

Will you give permission for a group picture to be taken?

Yes _____ No _____

## ■ Week 2: Telling My Story

The first session with the group lays the groundwork for the following sessions. Preschool children may never have been exposed to a group experience before. Indeed, some of the children may never have been in the company of strangers for any length of time. For these reasons, the primary goal of this session is to help the children feel comfortable with the group by getting to know each other and the facilitators. Make a special effort to connect with every child. Remember that it is doubtful whether children at this age level will ever be able to get beyond the parallel play stage during the course of the series. They may not necessarily become engaged with each other. That's why each child's relationship to the facilitator is of primary importance.

During this first session, the children are presented with many new concepts. They will be introduced to the series theme, the use of check-in, and the parameters of how the group runs. The facilitator will be doing a lot of talking this first session, however the children are given an opportunity to tell their story to each other. This is especially important, as the group gets to hear each child's version and understanding of his or her story which will help the facilitator to help the child and the caregivers grapple with misunderstandings or missing pieces in the story.

Lastly, the concept of "dead" is introduced to the children since it is central to the weeks that follow. Death is a concrete term and in the context of the group it is explained alone, unconnected to a certain set of spiritual beliefs. The spiritual aspects of death are better left to the child's family to explain. Should a child volunteer information about the family's spiritual beliefs, acknowledge that each family may have different ideas and encourage him or her to talk with the family about them. In group, give the child a simple, straightforward definition of death so that he or she has a good understanding of basic death concepts.

## Objectives

> To introduce group members to each other
> To define the word "dead" and introduce basic death concepts
> To share who died and how they died with group members

## Materials

| | |
|---|---|
| Cards: What Dies, What Doesn't | Me-sticks |
| Carpet squares | Name tags |
| Chuck, the Feeling Doll | Play-doh® |
| Coloring sheet: Some Things Die/ Some Things Don't | Play people (e.g., doctor, nurse, police officer, etc.) |
| Crayons | Play vehicles (e.g., ambulance, police car, etc.) |
| Dead things | Question cards |
| Feeling face cans | Question board |
| Felt balloon cut outs | Stickers |
| Flannelboard | Teddy bears |
| Koosh® ball | Toys |

## Procedures

### *Opening Activity*

#### Materials
Crayons
Name tags
Toys

As each child arrives, write his or her name on a name tag and attach it to him or her. The facilitator also should be wearing a name tag. Be certain to spell each child's name correctly and use the name he or she prefers. Sometimes, it is fun to allow children to draw or color on their name tags after their names have been written on them. These name tags are worn only for the first few weeks. Because the groups are limited in size, the children and facilitators usually learn each other's names after the first couple of weeks and then name tags are no longer necessary.

Given the age of these children, it is important for facilitators to be present and to welcome each child as he or she enters the room. Provide a few toys or games for those who arrive early.

Every week, to begin the session, sing the following song and teach the children the words. Then have the children stand in a circle, hold hands, and walk in a circle as the song is sung. The song is called I Like Me and is sung to the tune, Three Blind Mice.

> *I like me,*
> *I like me,*
> *No one is like me,*
> *No one is like me,*
> *You can look as far as the eye can see,*
> *Look behind every rock and tree,*
> *You'll never find anyone like me,*
> *Cuz' I am me.*

### *Getting to Know Each Other*

#### Materials
Carpet squares
Flannelboard with nine balloon cut outs
Koosh® ball
Teddy bears
(See Appendix 2 for balloon cut out template)

Have everyone sit in a circle facing each other on carpet squares. Facilitators introduce themselves again to the children and have them each say his or her name. Say, "we are going to meet each week for nine weeks. Each week we are going to take a balloon off of our board to help us count down the weeks. So let's take our first balloon off of the board and count how many balloons are left. 1–2–3–4–5–6–7–8 balloons left. That means we have eight more weeks left!"

Inform the children that everyone is in this group together because everyone has had a special person die. Then go around the circle and ask each child who the special person was that died and how he or she died.

Introduce the next activity by saying, "And now we are going to get to know each other more." Throw the ball to one of the children and ask him or her one of the following questions: What is your favorite food? favorite thing to do for fun? favorite TV show? favorite toy? Who is your best friend? Then that child throws the ball to another child who answers a different question, and so on until everyone has had a turn including the facilitators.

*Note:* Allow each child to be comfortable, while encouraging each to share with the group; be careful not to push too hard. This task will allow the children to know each other a little bit more and begin to establish communication and sharing among group members. Especially during the first week, some children may be shy or uncomfortable with the group, so be sensitive to these individual differences.

## Introducing Feelings

### Materials
Chuck, the feeling doll

The facilitator introduces the children to Chuck by explaining that each week Chuck will visit the group and share his feelings with them. Chuck has four feeling faces: happy, sad, mad, and scared. Show the children the four faces and have them guess what feelings the faces depict by saying things like. "Tonight Chuck is feeling happy because he gets to meet all of the children. Can someone find Chuck's happy face?"

## Sharing Feelings (Check-In)

### Materials
Feeling face cans
Me-sticks
(See Appendix 1 for a description of each item.
See Appendix 2 for sample feeling face cans)

Each child is given a Me-stick with his or her name on it. Show the children the feeling face cans. Ask, "Can you name the four feelings?" The four feelings are happy, sad, mad, and scared. Have the children put their Me-stick into the feeling face can that shows how they are feeling that night. As each child takes his or her turn, ask each child why he or she feels that way tonight. Chuck also has a Me-stick and checks in with the children. Tonight he is feeling happy because he is glad to be in the group with the children. Facilitators should check in, too.

*Note:* This checking-in activity occurs near the beginning of each session. This facilitates both identifying feelings and encouraging the children to focus on how they feel and on sharing these feelings with others. Again, be sensitive to the individual differences of the group members and do not force anyone to share.

## Sharing Our Stories

### Materials
    Question cards
    Question board
    (See Appendix 2 for sample question cards)

Following the check-in, each child is given an opportunity to tell more about his or her story about the special person who died. Explain this activity by saying, "now we are going to take some time to learn some more about the special person who died using the Question Board." Ask each child to remove a Question card from one of the squares on the Question Board, which covers one of the following questions:

Did you know he or she was going to die?
Who told you about the death and what did they tell you?
Were you with the person when he or she died? Tell us about that.
What do you remember about when the person died?
Did you go to the funeral? Tell us about that.
Was the body buried in the ground or cremated? What do you remember about that?
What time of day did the special person die?
Did you get to see the body of the person who died? Tell us about that.

Most children will be quite comfortable talking about these issues; this does not tend to be as 'heavy' an activity as it may be in an adult group. Therefore, when each child is answering the question, the facilitator should just be comforting and make appropriate comments to let each child know that he or she is listening.

*Note:* The above activity provides children with an opportunity to get to know each other better and talk about their loss with others. Recognize that other group members are likely to ask questions, and make it clear that each child may answer the questions if he or she is comfortable doing so, but no one is required to answer any questions. Again, be sensitive to the individual differences of the group members and do not force anyone to share.

## Take 5

By this time in the session, everyone needs a little break. It is a good idea to have everyone expend a little bit of energy during the break. Have each child touch the corresponding part of his or her body as everyone sings Head, Shoulders, Knees, and Toes:

*Head, shoulders, knees and toes, knees and toes,*
*head, shoulders, knees and toes, knees and toes,*
*eyes and ears and mouth and nose*
*head, shoulders, knees and toes, knees and toes.*

## Introduction to the Topic: What Does "Dead" Mean?

**Materials**
> Carpet squares
> Dead things (e.g. Flies, Bees, Flowers, or Taxidermy Animals)

Have children sit on their carpet squares. Explain, "tonight we are going to talk about the word "dead" and what that means." Reinforce that everyone in the group had a special person die; and everyone in the group had a special person die for different reasons. Say, "Now we're going to look at some dead things so that we can learn about what it means to be dead." Show the children a variety of "dead" things (dead bugs, flowers, etc.) and allow the children to touch them. Explore the following questions in an effort to facilitate the children's understanding of what "dead" means:

> "What does it mean to be dead?"
> > Allow each child to provide his or her ideas, correct inaccurate information, and answer questions they have.
> "How do you know each of these things is dead?"
> > It doesn't move, breathe, blink eyes; can't wake up, feel anything, talk, and so forth.
> "If something is dead, does it stay dead?"
> > Yes. When something is dead, it stays dead. It doesn't come back to life.
> "How do you think each of the things died?"
> > Bug: bug spray, life span; flower: it was picked, and so forth.
> "Do all living things die?"
> > Yes. All living things die.

Tell children that there are many reasons that living things die; "People and alive things such as plants and animals die for lots of reasons. Some of these reasons are illness, someone else hurts them, accident, injury, or old age."
> Reinforce these basic death concepts:

> Every living thing dies.
> Things, animals, and people die for different reasons.
> When someone or something dies, it stays dead.
> Death is not contagious. (Just because someone we know dies, it does not mean that we will die soon, too.)

## What Dies and What Doesn't?

**Materials**
> Cards, "What Dies, What Doesn't"
> (See Appendix 2 for sample cards)

Have children sit in a circle. Put the cards on the floor face down. Children take turns picking a card. When they pick a card they show it to the rest of the group. Then the facilitator asks, "Can a _____ die?" Children respond in unison, "Yes! A ____ can die" or "No! A _____cannot die." The facilitator also asks, "Why? Why can/can't a _____ die?" Children reply, "Because a ____ was/was not alive." The game continues until all of the children have had a turn. This exercise is a question/answer activity with a sing-song quality to it.

## Observed Play

**Materials**
 Coloring sheet: Some Things Die, Some Things Don't
 Crayons
 Play-doh®
 Play people
 Play vehicles
 (See Appendix 2 for the coloring sheet)

Each week at the end of the session, give children some time to choose between several activities. During this activity, continue to discuss children's understanding of what it means to be dead by using the coloring sheet and crayons. In addition, children may provide information about their loss experience in using the play people and play vehicles.

## Closing

The children stand in a circle, hold hands, and walk in a circle as they sing the same song that was used in the opening activity.

## A Reminder

**Materials**
 Stickers

Give each child a sticker at the conclusion of each session, to remind them of the group. See Appendix 3 for a sample note that can be given to caregivers each session.

# Week 3: Exploring Death

At the beginning of this session the children are introduced for the first time to the concept of centering. Centering may be unlike anything they have experienced before. For this reason, it may be difficult to convey to the children the need to be quiet and still. Helping the children to benefit from the full participation in a centering will take time and patience. One of the facilitators should narrate the centering while another one models for the children the kinds of behaviors that are expected for a centering.

This session builds on the concepts introduced in the second session. The children are introduced to the Denny the Duck story and they are given an opportunity to act out a funeral through the burial of Duane. This acting out brings the funeral rites down to a level that they can grasp and understand. It also can serve to help the children connect to Denny as he deals with the death of his friend, just as they grapple with the death of a special friend. The funeral affords the facilitator a chance to define the terms that the children may have heard at the time of the funeral such as *funeral, cemetery, casket*. In this way, the facilitators can clear up any misconceptions the children may have about the funeral rites.

## Objectives

> To build group cohesion
> To review the term "dead"
> To define terms related to the funeral and burial (e.g., bury, casket, cemetery, etc.)

## Materials

Carpet squares
Casket
Centering activity overview
Chuck, the Feeling Doll
Coloring sheet: Duane's Funeral
Crayons
Cremation ashes
Dead things
Denny the Duck
Duane the Duck
Feeling face cans
Felt balloon cut outs

Flannelboard
Flowers
Glossary of funeral terms
Gravestone
Me-sticks
Picture of cemetery and casket
Plastic sheet
Play people
Sandbox
Stickers
Story: *The Story of Denny the Duck*
Teddy bears

## Procedures

### *Opening Activity*

Use the same procedures outlined in Week 2.

## Centering Activity

### Materials
Centering Activity Overview
Carpet squares
(See Appendix 2 for the Centering Activity Overview)

Children are invited to find a place to lie on the floor on their carpet squares where they are not touching anyone. One of the facilitators narrates the centering activity. Other facilitators model for the children what to do during a centering exercise.

## Sharing Feelings (Check-In)

### Materials
Chuck, the Feeling Doll
Feeling face cans
Flannelboard with eight balloon cut outs
Me-sticks
(See Appendix 2 for sample feeling face cans and a balloon cut out template)

Use the same procedures outlined in Week 2. In addition, say, "Chuck is feeling happy again tonight because he gets to be with all of you. How do you know that Chuck is feeling happy? How do you act when you are feeling happy?"

Explain, "Now we are going to take another balloon down and count how many balloons are left. 1–2–3–4–5–6–7. We have seven more weeks left of group."

## Review of the Word "Dead"

### Materials
Dead things

Say, "Remember last week we talked about the word 'dead'? Who can tell me how we know if something is dead? Let's look at this dead bug. How do we know if the bug is dead?" Only a few items are necessary for this review.

Reinforces these basic death concepts:

Every living thing dies.
Things, animals, and people die for different reasons like illness, accidents, and old age. Sometimes we don't know why someone dies.
When someone or something dies, it stays dead.
Death is not contagious (Just because someone close to us dies, it does not mean that we will die soon, too.)

### Story: "Denny The Duck"

**Materials**
    Carpet squares
    Denny the Duck
    Story: *The Story of Denny the Duck* (See Appendix 6)

Children sit on their carpet squares. The facilitator explains, "Tonight we are going to meet Denny the Duck." Facilitator shows Denny to the children and explains, "Every week we are going to read a story about Denny the Duck. Tonight we will learn about Denny and his friend Duane." Once the story is read, ask the following questions:

> How did Duane the Duck die?
> How did Denny know that Duane was dead?
> Who came to Duane's funeral?
> What grows by Duane's grave?

## Take 5

Sing a song, selected from the appendices (e.g. "Tony Chestnut"):

> *To- (point to toe)*
> *ny (point to knee)*
> *Chest- (point to chest)*
> *nut (point to head)*
> *knows (point to nose)*
> *I (point to eye)*
> *love (cross arms over heart)*
> *you (point outward)*
> *Repeat 2 times, then*
> *I (point to eye)*
> *love (cross arms over heart)*
> *you (point outward).*

### Introduction To The Topic: Exploring Funeral Proceedings

**Materials**
    Casket
    Cremation ashes
    Duane the Duck
    Flowers
    Glossary of funeral terms
    Picture of cemetery and casket
    Plastic sheet
    Sandbox
    Tombstone
    (See Appendix 2 for the glossary of funeral terms and a sample tombstone)

Before doing this activity, review the Glossary of Funeral Terms. In group explain, "Now we will have a funeral for Duane." Ask the following:

Does anyone know what a funeral is? Did anyone go to a funeral?
> Explain that a funeral is a time when other people come to visit the family of the dead person to express their feelings about the person who died. "It is a time when we remember the person who died and a time when we can say good-bye to that person. A funeral is also a time when the dead body is buried or the person's ashes are buried." Children are taken to the sandbox. The facilitator explains that when a body is buried, the body is placed in a casket. The facilitator places Duane into the casket. The facilitator explains what a casket looks like and shows the children the picture of a casket.

Did any of your special people have a casket?
> When someone dies and his or her body is in the casket, people talk about that person and say good-bye.

Does anyone want to say something to Duane?
> The facilitator encourages the children to say good-bye to Duane and then closes the lid of the casket. "Remember that when a person's body is dead, it doesn't breathe and it doesn't feel any pain, so it won't hurt Duane to be in the box with the lid on it. Some people are buried in the ground in a place called a cemetery. A cemetery is a place where dead bodies are buried in the ground."

Did anyone go to the cemetery?
> The facilitator shows the children a picture of a cemetery.

Did the cemetery your special person is buried in look like the one in the picture?
> The facilitator explains that children can dig a hole in the sand for Duane's casket. Then Duane's casket is placed in the sand and covered. "After someone is buried, people often put a stone by the grave with the person's name on it and the day he or she was born and the date he or she died." The facilitator puts Duane's grave stone on Duane's grave.

Does anyone one what 'cremated' means?
> The facilitator points out that some people are cremated. "Cremation means that the dead body is put into a very hot oven and turned into ashes. This oven gets about three times as hot as the oven in your home. Since a dead body doesn't feel any pain, cremation doesn't hurt." Show the children some cremation ashes and try to elicit questions, concerns, and comments from the children.

Review the words learned today including: casket, gravestone, dead, cemetery, funeral, bury, and cremation. Remind the children that it is important to ask questions if there is anything they do not understand about the death or the funeral.

## *Observed Play*

**Materials**
   Coloring sheet: Duane's Funeral
   Crayons
   Denny and Duane
   Play people
   Sandbox
   (See Appendix 2 for the coloring sheet "Duane's Funeral")

As children play, talk with them about the topic for the evening and how it relates to the their own experiences. For instance, using the coloring sheet, ask questions about each child's experience or memories of the funeral. Additionally, children may use the sandbox and play people to communicate their funeral experiences.

## *Closing*

Use the same procedures and song as outlined in Week 2.

Reinforce that "when someone dies we need to keep asking questions to someone we can trust. We need to get our questions answered."

## *A Reminder*

**Materials**
   Stickers

Use the same procedures outlined in Week 2.

# ■ Week 4:  Identifying Changes

This session addresses the myriad of changes that occur after the death of a special person. Preschool children are probably the most sensitive to the changes in a home after a death since their world is so small and they depend on the adults around them for their care. Although death is a concrete subject, children may not make the connection between the death and the changes that they are experiencing and feeling. This session helps them to make that connection and challenges their magical thinking that they may have caused these changes in their lives. The children are introduced to the concept of change as they explore the world around them and the things that change in nature and in their daily lives.

Denny the Duck, in the story *Life After Duane*, presents the concepts of change as it relates to the death of a special person. After the children read the story, they are given an opportunity through play dolls and an imaginary house to identify the changes in their own families and in themselves since the death. In this way, the session helps to define for them not only the global changes that are part of all human experience, but also the profound life altering changes that come with the death of a special person in their own lives.

## Objectives

To define the word "change"
To identify different types of change
To identify changes in the child's family since the loss
To identify personal changes since the loss

## Materials

Carpet squares
Centering activity overview
Change cards
Change circles, bag
Change mittens
Change pictures
Chuck, the Feeling Doll
Coloring sheet: Life After Duane (4 choices)
Crayons
Family of dolls

Feeling face cans
Felt balloons
Flannelboard
Furniture
Me-sticks
Play-doh®
Shoeboxes
Stickers
Story: *Life After Duane*
Teddy bears

## Procedures

### *Opening Activity*

Use the same procedures outlined in Week 2.

### *Centering Activity*

**Materials**
　　Carpet squares
　　Centering Activity Overview
　　(See Appendix 2 for the Centering Activity Overview)

Use the same procedures outlined in Week 3.

### *Sharing Feelings (Check-In)*

**Materials**
　　Chuck, the Feeling Doll
　　Feeling face cans
　　Flannelboard with seven balloon cut outs
　　Me-sticks
　　(See Appendix 2 for sample feeling face cans
　　　　and a balloon cut out template)

Use the same procedures outlined in Week 2. Chuck checks in, too. Tonight he is feeling scared. Can the children find the scared face on Chuck? What do they think makes Chuck scared? Ask, "How do we know if someone is scared? How do people act when they feel scared?" (They may shake, sweat, laugh, bite their nails, suck their thumbs, etc.)

　　Explain, "Now we are going to take another balloon down and count how many balloons are left. 1–2–3–4–5–6. We have six more weeks left of group."

## *Introduction To The Topic: What Is Change?*

**Materials**
   Change mittens
   Change pictures
   (See Appendix 2 for change mittens and change pictures)

Ask:

>   What is change?
>       Change means that something is different. There are many things all around us
>       that change. Some changes in our lives we can make change (like what we wear,
>       how we wear our hair, our feelings, etc.). Other things we cannot change.
>   Can you make the weather change?
>       No. We don't have anything to do with what kind of weather we have. It changes
>       all by itself.
>   Can any of you make it snow or make the weather get cold?
>       No. Those are changes that we can't change.
>   What happens to you every day that you cannot control or change?
>       You grow. Your bodies change every day and you are not making that happen.
>       As you get older, your body grows and changes. If you eat food and get exercise,
>       your body will continue to grow until you are an adult and then your body quits
>       growing. Your body grows and you are not making that change; it happens
>       naturally.

Tell the children, "Another thing that you did not make change is that your special person died. We cannot change that they have died. We did not make them die. And we cannot make them come back alive. That is one change that has happened to us that we did not make happen. It was beyond our control."

*Note:* Many children feel guilty about the loss. Emphasize that the loss was not their fault, that they could not change the loss.

"Let's see if we can find some changes around the room." All around the room there are small paper mittens that are hidden. Let's see how many mittens we can find." Once all of the mittens are found, the children should take the pictures out of the pocket in each mitten. Explain that all of the mittens have changes in them (on the pictures) that the children should try to match (e.g., an egg and a chicken; a caterpillar and a butterfly; day and night, etc.). Once all of the pictures are matched, point out the different changes to the children.

"Change is all around us, and it is a part of our lives. But when someone dies there can be lots of changes that are very hard for us. Tonight we will talk about these changes."

## Story

**Materials**
    Carpet squares
    Story: *Life After Duane* (See Appendix 6)

Children sit on carpet squares as the facilitator reads the story. After the facilitator has read the story, ask,

> Name some things that changed for Denny after Duane died?
> Have you had any of these changes since your special person died?

## Take 5

Say, "Now we are going to play a game where we are going to change ourselves."
    Children will change themselves in two ways. Do the following exercises with the children to model what to do.

> Children pretend to be baby kangaroos in their mothers' pouches. Children scrunch up like they are in their mothers' pouches where it is dark and warm and cozy. Now they begin to crawl out of the pouches like they are climbing a wall. They take their arms out first, then their legs, and then fall onto the floor. They get up slowly and hop a small hop. Then they hop two hops, and then they hop all over the room.
> Children pretend to be a kernel of corn popping into popcorn. First they lay in the bottom of the pan, then they begin to sizzle by moving all over the pan and then they begin to POP! "Who will pop first?" When they pop, they jump up, and keep jumping until all the "corn" has popped! Then they will have a shower of salt and butter. "Ooooh! That feels good!"

## Life Is Changing: Family Changes

**Materials**
    Family of dolls
    Shoeboxes
    Dollhouse furniture

*Note:* Use ethnically appropriate dolls (i.e., African American, Asian American, European American, etc.), depending on your group's participants.
    Explain, "When someone dies, there are lots of changes that happen in our families. We're going to spend some time talking about some of the changes that you've experienced since the death." Show the children several boxes that look like rooms in a house and explain that all houses are different. "Some people live in an apartment, others live in a mobile home, others live in a house."

"How should we make our house?" Children help to create the shape of the house. Each of these boxes has furniture in it to depict different kinds of rooms. There will be a living room, a kitchen, two bedrooms, and a bathroom. The facilitator talks about the family that lives there by showing them the doll figures and telling them about the family.

The facilitator then takes one of the child doll figures and places them in one of the rooms and describes the way it used to be (e.g., "before Mom died she always cooked dinner. After she died, we always eat takeout"). Then the special person is removed from the room leaving only the child (or other family members). The facilitator then describes for the children what has changed.

These might be some changes:

Kitchen
    Special person doesn't eat with them anymore
    Eat different food
    People don't eat as much
    Empty chair at the table
    Don't sit at the table anymore
Bedroom
    Don't get tucked in by the special person anymore
    Can't fall asleep
    Scared of the dark now
    Has nightmares
Living Room
    Family doesn't have fun anymore
    No one talks to each other anymore
    Kids watch a lot more TV
    People fight more
    Don't get to see the person who died anymore
Bathroom
    Sometimes the child has toileting accidents
    Someone else gives child a bath
Outside the House
    Family doesn't play outside anymore
    Have to go to a babysitter now
    Don't get to play with the special person anymore

Reinforce that even though the children may not live in houses that looks like the one in group, each one of them have had a special person die and there have been many changes at their house since that person died. Many of these changes are in different rooms of their own homes.

## Change Game

### Materials
Change cards
Change circles [in a bag]
(See Appendix 2 for Change Cards and Change Circles)

Teach the children the song: Life is Changing All Around to the tune, London Bridge:

> *Life is changing all around,*
> *All around,*
> *All around,*
> *Life is changing all around,*
> *Everything is different.*

Children play an adapted version of London Bridge using the above song. Children get in a line, then pass under the arched arms of the facilitators, singing as they go. When the song ends, the arched arms of the facilitators come down and catch a child under the bridge. Whoever is caught in the bridge picks a colored circle from a bag. Each color represents a different room in the house. The child then chooses a card of the corresponding color. The facilitator reads what is on the card and asks if the child has experienced this change since their loss. If the child has, then the facilitator may ask the child about that change (e.g., How has it been since that change?; How do you feel about the change?; How do you do things now?). Ask the other children if they have had that change. Then the children continue with the game until everyone has had a turn.

Conclude this section by reinforcing that "lots of changes can happen in a home after a special person dies."

## Observed Play: Play-doh and Changes

### Materials
Coloring sheet: Life After Duane (4 sheets)
Crayons
Play-doh®
(See Appendix 2 for the coloring sheets)

Children should be given a choice of Play-doh® or coloring materials. Suggest that they change the Play-doh®. Some changes might be making a ball, making a pancake, making a snake, poking it, making it look like a donut, and so forth. This gives the children a chance to relax and also provides the facilitators with an opportunity to watch the children as they engage in these activities. These activities may yield additional information about what the child is thinking.

## *Closing*

Use the same procedures outlined in Week 2.

Reinforce that when someone dies there are lots of changes in a family and even though there are many changes, "it is still a family."

## *A Reminder*

### Materials
Stickers

Use the same procedures outlined in Week 2.

Tell the children to bring a picture of their special person and anything that either belonged to them or reminds them of their special person next week. Include this information in the note that is sent home to caregiver.

# ■ Week 5: Memories/Remembering

This session helps group members get in touch with the memories they have of their special people. Group members are asked to bring in a picture and something that reminds them of their special person. This activity is the centerpiece of the session. The children are asked to sit on a special memory chair and they are given a memory crown to wear while they are showing what they have brought. Each child can then take a crown home with him or her. The emphasis on the memory chair and crown is meant to communicate to the children that we place importance on memories and that re-membering is a special aspect of mourning. It also helps each child feel special.

The children hear another story about Denny the Duck, as he remembers Duane, and are asked to talk about the memories that they have of their special person. Lastly, the forget-me-not tray activity is used to illustrate that even though the children have lost the physical presence of their special person in their lives, they can still remember them in their hearts; that part of them will never go away.

## Objectives

To define the word "memory"
To discuss the importance of memories
To share pictures and belongings of the deceased special persons
To recall good memories

## Materials

Carpet squares
Centering activity overview
Chuck, the Feeling Doll
Coloring sheet: Denny Remembers Duane
Crayons
Feeling face cans
Felt balloon cut outs
Flannelboard
Forget-me-not tray with items
Memory candles (matches)

Memory chair
Memory crowns
Me-sticks
Nerf® ball
Pictures/belongings of special people
Sheet
Stickers
Story: *A Duck Never Forgets*
Taper candle
Teddy bears

## Procedures

### *Opening Activity*

Use the same procedures outlined in Week 2.

### *Centering Activity*

**Materials**
  Carpet squares
  Centering Activity Overview
  (See Appendix 2 for the Centering Activity Overview)

Use the same procedures outlined in Week 3.

### *Sharing Feelings (Check-In)*

**Materials**
  Chuck, the Feeling Doll
  Feeling face cans
  Flannelboard with six balloon cut outs
  Me-sticks
  (See Appendix 2 for sample feeling face cans and a balloon cut out template)

Use the same procedures outlined in Week 2. Chuck also checks in. Tonight Chuck is feeling sad. "What makes you sad? How do you act when you are sad? Can you always tell if someone is sad by looking at him or her?"

Explain, "Now we are going to take another balloon down and count how many balloons are left. 1–2–3–4–5. We have 5 more weeks left of group!"

### *Introduction To The Topic: What Is A Memory?*

Explain, "Tonight we are going to talk about memories. Does anyone know what a memory is? A memory is like walking backward in your mind. It means that you re-member something—something that you did or someone that you knew. When a special person dies, we don't have them with us anymore, but we may have memories of the person or things we did with him or her. Tonight we are going to try to remember memories about your special person who died."

"It's important to talk about our special person who died and to remember him or her so that we don't forget him or her. If we keep remembering our special person who died, we can keep the memory of that person inside of us forever."

## *Sharing Our Memories*

**Materials**
Memory chair
Memory crown
Pictures/belongings of special people
(See Appendix 2 for memory crown template)

Children share the pictures and belongings they brought of their special person. Each child takes a turn showing what he or she brought. Each child sits in the memory chair and wears a memory crown as he or she shares. Have the children pass the things as the child talks about them. Ask questions such as, "Do you remember when that picture was taken?; What do you remember about when you got this (item)?, and so forth. Remind the children to be careful with each others' things.

## *Take 5*

**Materials**
Nerf® ball
Sheet—"Who You Gonna Call?"
(See Appendix 2 for the sheet)

Have children stand in a circle and hold the sheet. Then throw the ball into the middle of the sheet and have the children move the sheet up and down as quickly as they can. The object is to keep the ball on the sheet.

## *Story*

**Materials**
Carpet squares
Story: *A Duck Never Forgets* (See Appendix 6)

Have children sit on their carpet squares. Read the story to them and then ask the following questions:

What memory of Duane made Denny laugh?
What memory of Duane made Denny cry?
What is something that Duane taught Denny?
What is something that Denny never wants to forget about Duane?
What is one memory with Duane that only Denny and Duane share?

### Forget-Me-Not Activity

**Materials**
Forget-Me-Not Tray

Introduce this activity by saying, "Since we are talking about memories tonight, we're going to see how good you all are at remembering things." Show the children the forget-me-not tray. On the tray place several different small items. Name and point out each item. Ask the children to close their eyes. Remove one of the items from the tray. Have the children open their eyes, look at the tray, and try to guess what item is missing.

At the conclusion of this activity, reinforce that even though things were missing from the tray, the children could remember those things. They were no longer in sight, but everyone remembered what those items were. "That's the way it is when a special person dies. Even though we don't get to see them or touch them anymore we still remember them, and we still remember what they were like."

### Memory Candles Activity

**Materials**
Memory candles (Matches)
Taper candle

Children sit on their carpet squares. Place a tea light or heart candle in front of each child (turn down the lights) and explain, "Now we are going to light these candles to remember our special person." Light the taper candle, then go around and light each child's candle. As it is lit, each child says, "I remember (name the special person that died)."

*Note:* Group facilitators must be very careful and responsible when young children are handling the candles, considering the children's age and energy level.

### Observed Play

**Materials**
Crayons
Coloring sheet: Denny Remembers Duane
(See Appendix 2 for coloring sheet)

This portion of the session gives the children a chance to relax and also provides the facilitators an opportunity to watch the children as they engage in assorted activities. For instance, when coloring the specified sheets, on what does the child focus (e.g., do they draw additional items on the coloring sheet related to their personal experience?). These activities may yield additional information about what the child is thinking.

## *Closing*

Use the same procedures outlined in Week 2.

Reinforce that when someone dies we still have our memories of them and these will likely never go away.

## *A Reminder*

**Materials**

Stickers

Use the same procedures outlined in Week 2.

# ■ Week 6: Identifying and Expressing Feelings

The goal for this session is two-fold: to help the children identify and label their feelings around the death and to validate their feelings. Through check-in the children have learned how to label the four basic feelings. Now they are being asked to relate these feelings to their experience of the death. No judgments are made about the feelings that they have or how they express them. Here, the focus of the session is only to identify and label the feelings and to talk about how they express them. In this way, they can make the connection between their feelings and the death as well as the feelings of others around them and the death. Week eight will teach them ways to cope with their feelings.

## Objectives

To define the word "feelings"
To identify different types of feelings and share these feelings
To identify feelings around death and the expression of these feelings

## Materials

Bubbles
Carpet squares
Centering activity overview
Chuck, the Feeling Doll
Coloring sheet: I am Full of Feelings
Crayons
Feeling face cans
Feeling masks

Felt balloon cut outs
Flannelboard
Handout: How Would You Feel If
Me-sticks
Play-doh®
Stickers
Story: *A Duck Has Feelings, Too!*
Teddy bears

## Procedures

### *Opening Activity*

Use the same procedures outlined in Week 2.

### *Centering Activity*

**Materials**
Carpet squares
Centering activity overview
(See Appendix 2 for centering activity overview)

Use the same procedures outlined in Week 3.

### Sharing Feelings (Check-In)

**Materials**
　　Chuck, the Feeling Doll
　　Feeling face cans
　　Flannelboard with five balloon cut outs
　　Me-sticks
　　(See Appendix 2 for sample feeling face cans and a balloon cut out template)

Use the same procedures outlined in Week 2. Chuck checks in, too. Tonight he is feeling mad. A child is asked to find the mad face for Chuck. "What makes Chuck mad?" "How do you know Chuck is feeling mad?"

　　Explain, "Now we are going to take another balloon down and count how many balloons are left. 1–2–3–4. We have four more weeks left of group."

### Introduction To The Topic: What are Feelings?

**Materials**
　　Bubbles

Ask,

> What is a feeling?
> 　A feeling is something we think or a way that we act about something that has happened.
> Can you name some feelings?
> 　Happy, sad, mad, scared . . .
> How do we know what someone is feeling?
> 　We may know by how they look and by how they act or by what they say.
> Do we always know what someone is feeling by looking at him or her?"
> 　No. Sometimes people hide their feelings.
> Do we always know what we are feeling or why we are feeling that way?
> 　No. Sometimes we don't know what we are feeling. Other times we may know that we are feeling bad, but we may not know why.
> Can two people feel differently about the same thing?
> 　Yes.
> How does someone act when they are sad? mad? happy? scared?

Begin to blow some bubbles. Say that "feelings are a lot like bubbles. Some bubbles pop quickly, others last a long time. Some feelings come and go quickly, others last a long time. Some bubbles are big and some bubbles are small. That's how feelings are: some are big and some are small. When we have a special person die, some of our feelings can be big feelings and they last a long time."

　　Children can now blow bubbles for little while.

### *Feelings Movement Activity*

Say these lines and do the body movements. The entire group can repeat this activity several times.

> *I am full of feelings (hug self)*
> *That are trying to get out (spread arms quickly)*
> *Sometimes when I'm feeling*
> *I want to cry (cry) or shout (shout)*
> *It's good to feel our feelings (one thumb up)*
> *It's good to get them out (other thumb up)*
> *Happy, sad, scared, and mad*
> *Are what feelings are about!*

## *Story*

### Materials

Carpet squares
Story: *A Duck Has Feelings, Too!* (See Appendix 6)

Children sit on carpet squares as the story is read. After, ask the children these questions:

> What kinds of feelings did Denny have after Duane died?
> How did he show his feelings?
> Have you had any of these feelings since your special person died?
> How do you show your feelings?

## *Take 5*

Sing the song, When You're Happy and You Know It:

> *When you're happy and you know it, clap your hands (clap twice)*
> *When you're happy and you know it, clap your hands (same)*
> *When you're happy and you know it, then your body sure will show it,*
> *When you're happy and you know it, clap your hands (clap twice)*

### Verse 2

> *When you're sad and you know it cry boo-hoo (say "boo-hoo," with a whiny voice and sad face)*

### Verse 3

> *When you're scared and you know it, shake, shake, shake (shake all over)*

### Verse 4

> *When you're mad and you know it, stomp your feet (stomp your feet)*

## *How Would You Feel If?*

**Materials**
  Feeling face masks
  Handout: How Would You Feel If?
  (See Appendix 2 for sample feeling face masks and handout)

"Now we are going to use masks to talk about feelings." Give each child four masks, one for each feeling (happy, sad, mad, and scared). The children are asked to name the masks. Then tell the children that he or she is going to describe a situation and they have to think about how they would feel about it: "Let's think about what feelings we have in different circumstances." When they have picked a feeling, they are to put the mask that corresponds to how they might feel in front of their faces: "Hold up the masks that show how you might be feeling." Select statements from the "How Would You Feel If?" handout (e.g., how would you feel if someone broke your favorite toy, etc.). Each child will hold up the mask that depicts how he or she might feel. If the question picked is not applicable, they may pick a new one.

Comment on the different masks the children have picked for each statement. Reinforce that each child may have shown different feelings for different times of the day. "Feelings are with us all of the time, when we sleep, when we wake up, when we eat, when we are in the car, when we play with friends, and when we go to bed."

## *Observed Play*

**Materials**
  Bubbles
  Crayons
  Coloring sheet: I Am Full of Feelings
  Play-doh®
  (See Appendix 2 for coloring sheet)

This portion of the session allows the children to unwind, and also provides the facilitators an opportunity to watch the children as they engage in assorted activities. For instance, when coloring the specified sheets, what feeling(s) does the child focus on? Also, facilitators can reexplore feelings while the children play with the bubbles. These activities may yield additional information about what the child is thinking.

## *Closing*

Use the same procedures outlined in Week 2.

Reinforce that "we all have many feelings (sad, mad, happy, and scared) and when a special person dies our feelings can last a long time."

## *A Reminder*

### Materials
Stickers

Use the same procedures outlined in Week 2.

# ■ Week 7: Exploring Unfinished Business

This session focuses on unfinished business, a concept that may be difficult for children this age to grasp. The story of Denny the Duck: I Never Got to Say Good-Bye helps the children to understand what is meant by unfinished business. Children at this level may not be able to explore this topic to the depth of older children or their parents or caregivers, but they can understand the sense of responsibility they may feel for the death of their special person; they therefore need to be reassured that they had nothing to do with the death. They can also understand that they will not be able to do certain things with their special person any more. They need an opportunity to talk about these things. At the end of the session the children will dictate a love note to one of the facilitators so that they can say what they want to say to their special person. A note is sent home with the caregivers explaining the love notes and how the caregivers can help the children decide what to do with them. This activity draws the caregiver into the child's need to communicate with his or her special person and helps the caregivers to understand the importance of keeping that link for the child.

## Objectives

To discuss the things we didn't get to do with our special person
To say what we didn't get to say to our special person
To share anything about the death that remains troubling

## Materials

Carpet squares
Centering activity overview
Chuck, the Feeling Doll
Coloring sheet: Denny Misses Duane
Crayons
Feeling face cans
Felt balloon cut outs
Flannelboard
Koosh® ball

Love notes
Me-sticks
Pens
Play-doh®
Question cards and container
Stickers
Story: *Denny Says Good-Bye to Duane*
Teddy bears
Unfinished business slips on felt stars

## Procedures

### Opening Activity

Use the same procedures outlined in Week 2.

## Centering Activity

### Materials
Carpet squares
Centering activity overview
(See Appendix 2 for centering activity overview)

Use the same procedures outlined in Week 3.

## Sharing Feelings (Check-In)

### Materials
Chuck, the Feeling Doll
Feeling face cans
Flannelboard with four balloon cut outs
Me-sticks
(See Appendix 2 for sample feeling face cans and a balloon cut out template)

Use the same procedures outlined in Week 2. Tonight Chuck is feeling scared. One of the children finds the scared face for Chuck. "What makes you scared? How do you act when you are scared? Why is it important to tell someone when you are scared?"

Explain, "Now we are going to take another balloon down and count how many balloons are left. 1–2–3. We have three more weeks left of group."

## Introduction To The Topic: Exploring Unfinished Business

"Tonight we are going to talk about when your special person died."

How many of you got to say 'good-bye' to your special person *before* he or she died?
If a child did get to say good-bye, help him or her describe what happened.
How many of you got to say good-bye *after* your special person died?
Help children talk about ways they got to do that.

"Tonight we are going to talk about what it's like to never get to say good-bye to our special person. We're also going to talk about the things that we didn't get to do with our special person."

## Story

### Materials
Carpet squares
Story: *Denny Says Good-Bye to Duane* (See Appendix 6)

Have children sit in a circle on their carpet squares. Read the story, *I Never Got to Say Good-Bye*. After reading the story to the children, ask these questions:

What made Denny cry when he thought about Duane?

What were some of the things that Denny and Duane had planned to do with each other that they would not be able to do now?

How did Denny know that Duane would never be far away?

## Take 5

Play a fun game like Simon Says or Red Light/Green Light.

## Question Cards

**Materials**
Question cards and container
(See Appendix 2 for sample question cards)

Explain, "we are going to answer some questions from these cards." Each child selects a card from the container and then answers that question.

The purpose of this discussion is to give group members an opportunity to talk about these ideas with their peers.

## Exploring Unfinished Business

**Materials**
Flannelboard
Koosh® ball
Unfinished business slips on felt stars
(See Appendix 2 for unfinished business slips)

Children sit in a circle on their carpet squares. Explain, "When someone dies, sometimes we feel sad about all of the things we used to do with that person and all of the things we didn't get to do before he or she died. We're going to talk about some of those things now. First we're going to learn a new song. It is sung to the tune of London Bridge."

*I wish we could have*
*Wish we could*
*Wish we could*
*Wish we could*
*I wish we could have,*
*Wish we could*
*I wish we could have done it.*

Children pass the Koosh® ball around as they sing the song. When the music stops, whoever is holding the Koosh® ball picks a star from the flannelboard. The facilitator reads it and the child responds to what is on it (e.g., I wish I could have said good-bye). Keep doing this until everyone has had a turn.

### Love Notes

**Materials**
Love notes
Pens
(See Appendix 2 for sample love notes paper)

Remind children that some of them didn't get to say good-bye to their special person. Even if they did, they likely still have things they want to say to their special person. "We're going to think about what we would like to say to our special person and write that on a love note." Help the children write down what they would like to say. Then talk to the children about what they would like to do with their love notes. Do they want to take it with them to the cemetery? Do they want to take it home and put it in a special place? Do they want to have their other special people read it? Do they want to put it away as something to keep and remember about their special person?
*Note*: Include in the note home to caregivers what the love notes are about.

### Observed Play

**Materials**
Coloring sheet: Denny Misses Duane
Crayons
Play-doh®
(See Appendix 2 for coloring sheet)

This gives the children a chance to relax and also provides the facilitators an opportunity to watch the children as they engage in assorted activities. These activities may yield additional information about what the child is thinking.

### Closing

Use the same procedures outlined in Week 2.
Reinforce that even though a special person has died, the children can still talk to them and remember them.

### A Reminder

**Materials**
Stickers

Use the same procedures outlined in Week 2.

# ■ Week 8: Coping with Feelings

This session is intended to build on the concepts presented in Week 6. While that session was intended to help the children identify and label their feelings and the ways that they express them, this session is intended to help them learn healthy coping techniques. Use a balloon in the session to illustrate in a very concrete way what can happen if we don't let feelings out. As Denny the Duck learns how to deal with his feelings, the children learn from him as well. Finally, the mad targets help the children to express their anger. All of the activities are geared to illustrate to the children how they can cope with feelings in a healthy way.

Facilitators should meet with caregivers individually for about 10–15 minutes before or after this session to discuss the children's grief and current adjustment. In addition, you can discuss whether further participation of the youth is recommended or desired. Recommendations may be provided regarding appropriate bereavement services considering the current adjustment of the child and the primary caregiver's concerns.

## Objectives

> To identify reactions to feelings
> To identify feelings that trouble us
> To explore healthy ways to cope with our feelings

## Materials

Balloons
Carpet squares
Centering activity overview
Chuck, the Feeling Doll
Coloring sheet: Denny the Duck Learns
    About Feelings
Crayons
Feeling face cans
Felt balloon cut out
Flannelboard

Mad target
Me-sticks
Plastic sheet
Play-doh®
Stickers
Story: *Denny the Duck Learns
     About Feelings*
Teddy bears
Wet sponges

## Procedures

### *Opening Activity*

Use the same procedures outlined in Week 2.

## Centering Activity

**Materials**
    Carpet squares
    Centering activity overview
    (See Appendix 2 for centering activity overview)

Use the same procedures outlined in Week 3.

## Sharing Feelings (Check-In)

**Materials**
Chuck, the Feeling Doll
Feeling face cans
Flannelboard with three balloon cut outs
Me-sticks
(See Appendix 2 for sample feeling face cans and a balloon cut out template)

Use the same procedures outlined in Week 2. Tonight Chuck is feeling mad again. One of the children finds the mad face for Chuck. "What makes you mad? How do you act when you are mad? Why is it important to tell someone when you are mad?"

Explain, "Now we are going to take another balloon down and count how many balloons are left. 1-2. We have two more weeks left of group."

## Introduction To The Topic: Coping With Feelings

**Materials**
    Balloon

"Tonight we are going to talk about how to get our feelings out." Introduce the topic by telling the children, "It's not good to keep our feelings on the inside because they may build up and then come out stronger than they would if we would share them with someone. Sometimes when our feelings build up we express them in unhealthy ways, like beating up on someone, or putting someone down, or lying around the house, or not being able to sleep."

Illustrate this concept by using a balloon. "If we keep our feelings in, then the feelings will just build up like when we keep putting air into a balloon. If we keep putting air into a balloon, eventually it will pop, just like our feelings pop out of us if we don't get them out."

Ask the children to pretend to be a balloon. Have them take in air. As they take in more and more air ask, "Do you feel like you are going to explode?" Then have them let the air out slowly. Now ask if it feels better to let the air out? Say, "That's how it feels when we let our feelings out; it helps us feel better." End this activity by asking, "Do you remember how it felt when you held in all of the air and didn't let it out? That's how it is when we don't let our feelings out, when we try to keep them in. It's important to let our feelings out. Tonight we are going to learn healthy ways to express our feelings so that we don't end up hurting ourselves or others."

## Story

**Materials**
    Carpet squares
    Story: *Denny the Duck Learns About Feelings* (See Appendix 6)

Children sit on their carpet squares while the facilitator reads the story. After the story, ask these questions:

    Who helped Denny learn about feelings?
    What did he learn that will help him with his feelings?

## Take 5

"We're going to learn a song about what happens to our feelings if we don't get them out. It's called 'POP! Go My Feelings!' Listen to me sing it once and then you do it the second time." Crouch on the floor. At the 'POP,' jump up. What follows is the song, POP! Go My Feelings! to the tune: Pop! Goes the Weasel:

        *Every day, in every way,*
        *I have lots of feelings,*
        *If I don't get them out*
        *POP! Go My Feelings!*

    Sing the song at various speeds and volumes. Have children crouch and then pop up as they sing the song.

## Mad Targets

**Materials**
    Mad target
    Plastic sheet
    Wet sponges

Show the children the Mad Target. Explain, "Tonight we are going to get our anger out in a healthy way. Let's think of some things that make us mad." Model what to do before the children take their turn. Then each child takes a turn throwing a wet sponge at the target. As they hurl the sponge, they shout, "I am mad at . . . !" Each child may take several turns.

## Observed Play

**Materials**
Coloring sheet: Denny the Duck Learns About Feelings
Crayons
Play-doh®
(See Appendix 2 for coloring sheet)

This activity gives the children a chance to relax and also provides the facilitators an opportunity to watch the children as they engage in assorted activities. These activities may yield additional information about what the child is thinking.

## Closing

Use the same procedures outlined in Week 2.

## A Reminder

**Materials**
Stickers

Use the same procedures outlined in Week 2.

Tell children to bring their favorite stuffed animals or blankets to group next week. Also, tell them that the group picture will be taken next week. Include this information in the note that is sent home to caregivers.

# ■ Week 9: Learning Self-Care and Support

This session covers the concept of self-care and an important aspect of self-care—support. Children at this age are highly dependent on the adults around them to take care of them. When a family experiences the death of a special person, the children may not receive the same type of care they were used to; thus it is important to teach children self-care techniques. Time is spent focusing on the importance of self-care including eating right, playing, sleeping well, expressing feelings, and keeping their bodies clean. In terms of support, they learn, through the use of building blocks, what can happen if they don't have enough support in their lives. The children bring things that comfort them to the session to reinforce that even a stuffed animal can help us with our mourning. They also play a game that helps them to think about who they can go to for other kinds of support. Even children this young need help identifying key people in their lives who can give them support. The emphasis in this session is to get them to think about and name these people since they will need them as they move through their mourning.

Group pictures are taken tonight. Each child will be given a group picture at the last session to remind him or her of the support he or she got in the group.

Facilitators meet with caregivers individually for about 10–15 minutes before or after this session to discuss the children's grief and current adjustment. In addition, discuss whether further participation of the youth is recommended or desired. Recommendations may be provided regarding appropriate bereavement services considering the current adjustment of the child and the primary caregiver's concerns.

## Objectives

To define self-care and support
To discuss why self-care and support are important
To identify ways to provide self-care
To identify people who can provide support

## Materials

Blocks
Camera with film
Carpet squares
Cassette player, tape of Hokey Pokey
Centering activity overview
Chairs
Chuck, the Feeling Doll
Coloring sheet: I Have Help In
    My Own Pond
Crayons
Feeling face cans

Felt balloon cut outs
Flannelboard
Me-sticks
Self-care bag (with self-care items)
Sheet: Who You Gonna Call?
Stickers
Story: *Denny the Duck Finds Help in
    the Big Pond*
"Support" sign (to be put on one of
    the chairs)
Support friends
Teddy bears

## Procedures

### Opening Activity

Use the same procedures outlined in Week 2.

### Centering Activity

**Materials**
   Carpet squares
   Centering activity overview
   (See Appendix 2 for centering activity overview)

Use the same procedures outlined in Week 3.

### Sharing Feelings (Check-In)

**Materials**
   Chuck, the Feeling Doll
   Feeling face cans
   Flannelboard with two balloon cut outs
   Me-sticks
   Support friends
   (See Appendix 2 for sample feeling face cans and a balloon cut out template)

Use the same procedures outlined in Week 2. Chuck is feeling sad again tonight. "What makes Chuck sad? How does he act when he feels sad? Can we always tell when someone is sad?" As children check-in, they show what support friends they brought with them.

   Explain, "Now we are going to take another balloon down and count how many balloons are left. 1. We have 1 more week left of group. Next time will be our last time here."

### Introduction To The Topic: Learning Self-Care and Support

**Materials**
   Blocks

Explain, "Tonight we are going to talk about self-care and support." Introduce the topic of self-care with the following list of questions and comments:

   Does anyone know what self-care means?
      It means taking care of ourselves: our bodies, our minds, and our feelings so that we can grow up to be healthy and happy.  There are lots of ways we can take care of our bodies. One way to eat good food that helps us to grow. We can also get enough sleep.

Are there any other ways we can take care of our bodies?

Keep our bodies, hair, and teeth clean, get lots of exercise, and play in the fresh air. There are other ways we can take care of ourselves too. It's important that we play everyday. It's important to take care of our feelings. When we need help with our feelings, we need to tell someone how we feel so we get our feelings out.

Why is self-care so important?

With self-care, you will eat, sleep, look, and act better. You will be able to stay healthy and get the most out of life.

"When a special person dies, we need to make sure that we are taking care of ourselves so that we can stay healthy."

Say, "tonight we are going to learn ways to take care of ourselves."

Introduce the topic of support with the following question and comments.

Does anyone know what support means?

Support means help. When a special person dies, we need to take care of ourselves, but also we need to get support (or help) from others. When we have had a special person die, we need lots of help, including getting lots of hugs. When we need help with our feelings or other things that's called "support."

Illustrate the concept of support with blocks. "If we were going to try to build a tower with the blocks, what would happen to the tower if we kept putting blocks on top of each other?" Recruit children to help build the tower. Eventually the tower will fall over. "But if we give the tower more support, we can build a much stronger tower that will not fall over." Illustrate this concept by building a tower with a broader base.

"That's how it is for us when we need support. We cannot do it alone. We need other people to support us, give us help, so that we can keep on going. When we feel mad, sad, and scared, we need to tell other people how we feel. Sometimes our stuffed animals, toys, or pets can be our support friends. We can tell them how we feel. Can anybody think of anything or anyone else that is a support friend? Tonight we are going to learn ways to take care of ourselves and to get support."

## Take 5

**Materials**

Cassette player

Support friends

Tape, Hokey Pokey

Children do the Hokey Pokey with their support friends. Facilitators should model by bringing their own support friends and dancing with them.

## Who You Gonna Call?

**Materials**
Chairs
Sheet: Who You Gonna Call?
"Support" sign
(See Appendix 2 for sheet)

Chairs are arranged into two lines, back-to-back, like musical chairs. One chair has the "Support" sign on it. Explain, "We are going to play a game like musical chairs. We are going to march around these chairs while we chant: 'Who you gonna go to for some help? Who do you go to (pause) for help?' When the verse is finished, everyone sits in a chair." The facilitator reads one of the scenarios, listed on the sheet to the child sitting on the "support" chair. The child tells whom he or she would go to for help with that situation. Repeat several times until all of the children have had a turn in the Support chair.

Reinforce that it's good to know the people that the children can go to for help and that they will need to call on these people to help them during their sad, mad, or scared times.

## Self-Care Bag

**Materials**
Self-care bag
Items for self-care

Show the children a paper bag that contains various items. The things in the bag symbolize ways that the children take care of themselves (e.g., a hair comb, a bubble bath, an apple, etc.). Each child takes a turn picking an item out of the bag. The child then talks about how the item can help them take care of themselves. Each child should take a turn.

## Story

**Materials**
Carpet squares
Story: *Denny the Duck Finds Help in the Big Pond* (See Appendix 6)

Children sit on their carpet squares with their support friends as the story is read. After the story is read, ask these questions:

Who gave Denny support after Duane died?
Who gives the children support?

## *Observed Play*

**Materials**
    Blocks
    Coloring sheet: I Have Help In My Pond of Support
    Crayons
    (See Appendix 2 for coloring sheet)

This activity gives the children a chance to relax and also provides the facilitators an opportunity to watch the children as they engage in assorted activities. For instance, when coloring the specified sheets, what does the child focus on? These activities may yield additional information about what the child is thinking. For this coloring sheet, the children will need help to write the names of the people that they can turn to for support.

## *Closing*

**Materials**
    Camera with Film

Use the same procedures outlined in Week 2. Take the group picture.

## *A Reminder*

**Materials**
    Stickers

Use the same procedures outlined in Week 2.
    Remind the children that next week will be the last week of group.

# ■ Week 10: Learning to Say Good-Bye

This session helps the children say good-bye to each other and to the group experience. Another main goal of this session is to bolster their self-esteem. Each child is given a superstar medal for all of the hard work they did in the group. They have a small party and the session is more relaxed than previous sessions. The party and refreshments are intended to create some distance from the heaviness of the preceding weeks as the children disengage from the group. They are each given a Denny the Duck to remind them of the group, and also to remind them of the things that Denny taught them over the course of the group process. They know that as they leave the group with Denny, they are not alone. They have met other children just like them, and they have Denny to comfort them as they continue to mourn after the group has ended.

## Objectives

To identify personal gifts and strengths
To say good-bye to each other
To celebrate the group's last time together

## Materials

Carpet squares
Centering activity overview
Chuck, the Feeling Doll
Denny the Ducks (for each child)
Feeling face cans
Felt balloon cut outs
Flannelboard

Group pictures
Me-sticks
Snacks
Stickers
Stories: Denny the Duck stories
    (bring all 7 of them)
Superstar medals
Teddy bears

## Procedures
## Opening Activity

Use the same procedures outlined in Week 2.

## *Centering Activity*

**Materials**
Carpet squares
Centering activity overview
(See Appendix 2 for centering activity overview)

Use the same procedures outlined in Week 3.

## *Sharing Feelings (Check-In)*

**Materials**
   Chuck, the Feeling Doll
   Feeling face cans
   Flannelboard with on balloon cut out
   Me-sticks
   (See Appendix 2 for sample feeling face cans and a balloon cut out template)

Use the same procedures outlined in Week 2. Chuck also checks in. Tonight Chuck says good-bye to the children. Ask, "How do you think Chuck feels about saying good-bye to the group?" Allow children to express various ideas about how Chuck feels and have them tell the group why Chuck may feel that way.

   "Let's take our last balloon off of the board; we have no more weeks left of group."

## *Introduction To The Topic: Saying "Good-Bye"*

Explain, "Tonight is our last night of group and tonight we are going to spend some time saying good-bye to each other. We are going to remember all of the fun things we did together and all of things that we learned from Denny the Duck and each other."

## *"I Am A Superstar"*

**Materials**
   Superstar medals
   (See Appendix 2 for Superstar medal templates)

Tell the children that they are all very special and give each one of them a medal because "there is nobody like them in the whole world." Put the superstar medal around each child's neck, saying, "You are a superstar because . . . " The facilitator says what he or she likes about the child and should comment on progress over the course of the series, trying to describe behaviors rather than appearances. For example, "You are a superstar because you really listen well to the other kids;" or "You are a superstar because you tell people how you feel."

## *Take 5*

Perform this movement activity for the children as they watch. Do the activity again with the children. The facilitator may want to have the children do it more than once.

> *There's only one me (hold up one finger)*
> *In this whole world-wide (turn around)*
> *I love who I am (hug self)*
> *On the out and inside (touch head, toes, open arms, and bring them into body)*

## Snacks

**Materials**
  Appropriate Snacks
  Denny the Duck for each group member
  Group pictures
  Stories: Denny the Duck Stories (all 7 of them)

While having their snacks, everyone in the group should sit and talk about their favorite memories from the group. After everyone has shared everything, it is important to say good-bye again and talk about the ways that everyone will keep their memories of this group. "One way to keep our memories is to look at our pictures" (Hand out a group picture to each child).

Summarize the Denny the Duck stories. See Appendix 1 for a list of all the stories and a short description of each. Hand out a Denny the Duck to each child at this time.

## Closing

Use the same procedures outlined in Week 2.

## A Reminder

**Materials**
  Stickers

Use the same procedures outlined in Week 2. Make sure each child takes home a copy of the group picture.

*Note:* Following the final session a rememberance ceremony where the caregivers join their children can be held. This may include forming a circle and providing each person with a flower. Then, when the name of the deceased special person in announced, each person may place his or her flower in a vase in the center of the circle.

## ■ Resources

Jimerson, S. (1997). Jimerson—Grief Support Groups General Information Sheet (GIS). Available from the author.

# A Description of Materials

*Note:* The materials included with each level of the grief curriculum are designed to be developmentally appropriate; therefore, although the names of the materials may be the same, the materials differ slightly across the curriculum levels.

**Balloons:** It is best to use a medium size balloon (4–5 inches around). If the balloon is too large, it will take a long time to blow up and if it is too small, it will not hold much air. Also, it is wise to have multiple balloons with you (just in case of difficulty with the first balloon).

**Blocks:** In the session about self-care and support, the facilitator illustrates the concept of support with blocks. The facilitator, with help from the children, builds a tower of blocks to show that a tower with a strong broad base will not fall over as easily as one that has less support. The blocks are also used this session for the observed play. Standard wooden or plastic blocks are appropriate.

**Bubbles:** Purchase gallon bottles of bubbles and fill individual containers with the bubble solution, or make bubble solution from dishwashing soap and a small amount of sugar. Have individual containers and wands, so that the children can play with them after the discussion.

**Camera with Film:** A group picture is taken the second to last (9th) session. At the conclusion of week 10 each group member will be given a copy of the picture. Be sure to take a couple of pictures to insure a good shot. (see Group Picture below).

**Carpet Squares:** Carpet squares are used in the preschool group as a way to teach the children about personal space as well as giving them a special place to sit each week ("We should each sit on our own carpet square"). It also helps to keep the children in a circle. Local carpet stores are often very willing to donate carpet squares that are no longer carried in stock or they can be purchased relatively cheaply. Carpet squares are listed as a material each week for centering and story time.

**Casket:**  Use a small cardboard box just big enough for the Duane stuffed animal to fit in. Keep it simple or get elaborate as desired.

**Cassette Player and Tape, "Hokey Pokey":**  Any small cassette player will be sufficient. The Hokey Pokey tape is available at most stores that stock children's games or children's party items, or can be found at a local library. If it is not possible to use a cassette player and tape, sing the song.

**Centering Activity Overview:**  This is a script for guiding the children in a "centering" which is often used to begin the sessions. The script for leading the centering activity can be found in Appendix 2.

**Change Cards:**  Change cards describe various changes that can take place in different rooms of a house. Each room of change cards should be copied onto a different color of card stock paper, and these colors should correspond with the color chosen for the change circles for each room (described below). Once the change cards are copied, they should be laminated or covered with clear contact paper. Since preschool children cannot read, the facilitator should read the change written on the card to the child and ask the child if he or she has experienced that change since the death. Change cards can be found in Appendix 2.

**Change Circles:**  Change circles depict the different rooms in a house. Each change circle should be copied onto a different color of card stock paper, which corresponds with the color you choose for the change cards for each room (described above). A fabric bag can be used to put them in. When a child gets his or her turn, he or she picks a change circle from the bag. This change circle will correspond with a pile of change cards that are the same color and represent changes that can take place in a certain room in the house after a special person dies. Change circles can be found in Appendix 2.

**Change Mittens:**  The change mittens are used to hide the change pictures. Mittens are used in the winter, although there are other creative ways to hide the change pictures, for example, in small plastic Easter eggs. Whatever is used, put the change pictures (described below) in something so that they can be hidden throughout the room. The change mittens have a pocket in them to hold the change pictures. The change mittens should be copied onto card stock paper. A pattern for the change mittens (and change pictures) can be found in Appendix 2.

**Change Pictures:**  These pictures are used to introduce the concept of change to the children. These small pictures depict paired changes that are common in everyday life such as a chicken and an egg, a caterpillar and butterfly, day and night, a bud and a flower, a full glass and an empty glass, sun and rain, and two clocks showing different times of the day. The change pictures should be copied onto card stock paper and either laminated or covered with clear contact paper. For the activity, these cards are hidden (in change mittens, plastic eggs, etc.). The children search for and find the mittens, and then find the child who has the match to his or her picture. Once all of the pictures are matched, the facilitator points out the different changes to the children. Through this, the facilitator can reinforce the concept that things change around us all of the time, everyday. A pattern for the change pictures (and change mittens) can be found in Appendix 2.

**Chuck the Feeling Doll:** Chuck (the name given by the authors) is a life-sized fabric doll that is used in the preschool group. A local woman makes the dolls. The doll has four feeling faces: happy, sad, scared, and mad that velcro to his face. Chuck is used to teach the children about feelings and to model for them how to check-in and talk about feelings. The children can also hold him during group. Chuck the Feeling Doll can be purchased through the Centering Corporation. They are called "My Friends Dolls." Dolls can be ordered in Caucasian, Hispanic, African American, and Asian. They are $95.00. To order call the Centering Corporation at (402) 553-1200.

**Coloring Sheets:** Several weeks during the observed play section, children are given an opportunity to color a picture. The facilitators can chat with the children about their experience as they color the pictures. Coloring sheets can be found in Appendix 2.

   **"Duane's Funeral":** This coloring sheet includes the picture of Duane's Funeral from the story of Denny the Duck. This picture will remind children of different aspects of the funeral.

   **"Denny Misses Duane":** This coloring sheet includes the picture of Denny missing Duane from the story of Denny the Duck.

   **"Denny Remembers Duane":** This coloring sheet reminds children that although their special person is no longer here, they can still think about them.

   **"Denny The Duck Learns About Feelings":** This coloring sheet provides children with an opportunity to color the picture of Duane learning about feelings.

   **"I Am Full Of Feelings":** This coloring sheet helps children to identify their feelings. There are four different faces that the children can color. Below the faces are the words to the song "I am full of feelings."

   **"I Have Help In My Pond of Support":** This coloring sheet has the words "I Have Help In My Pond of Support" at the top. Under that, it has little ducks in a pond, and a place to write the names of people whom the child can turn to for support. The facilitator should ask the child who these people are and then write the names of the people for the child. The child can then color around the names and in the ducks. This allows the facilitator to examine who each child cites as his or her sources of support.

   **"Life After Duane":** This coloring sheet depicts four different changes that Denny experienced after Duane died. The children can choose which picture they would like to color.

   **"Some Things Die, Some Things Don't":** This coloring sheet reinforces the concept that only living things can die. One half of the sheets show pictures of things that can die; the other half of the sheet shows pictures of things that cannot die.

**Crayons:** Crayons are used frequently in the groups. They are much easier to use if they are put into Cool-whip or other plastic containers with covers rather than the boxes that the crayons come in. Having the crayons accessible in big containers allows the children to use them easily and relieves the hassle of getting the right crayons into the right box. Crayola now offers multicultural crayons with various skin tone shades. These are ideal, so that children of color can draw themselves. If multicultural crayons are not available, have the children draw on colored sheets of paper, such as blue or green, which neutralize the drawing surface. Never have children draw themselves on white paper, because this asks children of color to draw themselves as white.

**Cremation Ashes:** Some children in the group may have had their loved one cremated. Try to get some cremation ashes to show to the children. A large amount is not needed. The ashes helps the children to understand what we mean when we say that someone has been cremated.

**Dead Things:** Use dead things as a way to concretely explain the concept of "dead" or death. We collect dead things such as insects, flowers, worms, or animals that have been stuffed. There are two rules about dead things: Don't kill something in order for it to be dead, and don't use 'road kill.' The children will want to touch these dead things, so they tend to fall apart. For this reason, it is important to continue to collect things so there is always an ample supply. As a facilitator, take a matter-of-fact approach to these dead things and the children will be open to learning about death. If, however, the facilitator displays some reticence, the children will also be leery.

**Denny the Ducks:** Purchase small ducks at most novelty stores or children's stores. An alternative is to give each child an outline of Denny the Duck and have them color their own picture. Either way, this serves as a reminder of Denny the Duck and their participation in the support group.

**Dollhouse Furniture:** Purchase cheap dollhouse furniture to put into the various shoebox rooms. The children can decide what furniture they want to put into each room.

**Family of Dolls:** Purchase some playhouse dolls to depict different people in the family. Dolls that represent different cultures in order to be sensitive to all of the children in your group. Playskool® has sets of plastic dolls that represent various cultures. These dolls don't really fit into the shoeboxes, but they help the children talk about the different changes in the family after the death.

**Feeling Face Cans:** Feeling face cans are used for check-in. Focus on four feelings for check-in: happy, sad, mad, and scared, since these four feelings are the most easily teachable and recognizable for children. Make the cans out of soup cans, by covering the outside of them with construction paper. Make sure that there are no sharp edges on the can that the children could cut themselves on. A feeling face to represent each of the four feelings is put onto bright tagboard and either glued or taped onto the can. Samples of the feeling faces for the cans can be found in Appendix 2.

**Feeling Masks:** Trace a circle on tagboard and draw a feeling face on it. Cut out the circle and glue or tape it to a tongue depressor. Make one set of four feeling faces for every child in the group. Every child should have a happy, sad, mad, and scared face mask. Templates for feeling faces can be found in Appendix 2.

**Flannelboard with Balloons:** Since the preschool children have not acquired a good sense of time, use a flannelboard and some flannelboard pieces to count down the number of weeks in the series of groups. Either buy a flannelboard or buy some flannel at a fabric store and cover a piece of cardboard or wood with it. Then cut nine pieces out of felt to put on the flannelboard. Flannelboard pieces may symbolize a certain time of year, such as snowflakes for winter or apples for fall. Or, flannelboard pieces may be used that go along with a theme. Each flannelboard piece has a number on it (1–9), and is put on the flannelboard. Each week at the beginning of group, the flannelboard piece with the highest number is removed from the flannelboard and the children count down how many weeks of group are left. A balloon pattern for the flannel piece can be found in Appendix 2.

**Flowers:** Use artificial flowers that the children can lay at the gravesite of Duane in the sandbox. Ask for a volunteer to lay the flowers on the grave.

**Forget-Me-Not Tray:** Take a tray and add several small ordinary objects to it such as a pencil, brush, toothbrush, stuffed animal, spoon, and anything else desired. The children will look at the tray and, then close their eyes as the facilitator removes one item. The children will then look at the tray again and try to figure out what item has been removed, by remembering its original contents.

**Glossary of Funeral Terms:** This sheet includes definitions of the most common words a child is most likely to hear at the time of a funeral. Use these definitions to reenact a funeral after Duane's death. The glossary can be found in Appendix 2.

**Grief Support Groups General Information Sheet (GIS):** The GIS (Jimerson, 1997) is a list of questions to be used by the facilitator as a semi-structured interview during the Week 1 information interviews with the caregivers and children present. It provides the facilitators with some information about the child before the group begins, including information about the child's school, relationships, his or her relationship to the deceased, and so forth. A GIS is filled out for each individual child. A copy of the questions are included in the text of the Week 1 session, and an additional GIS, for photocopying, is included in Appendix 2.

**Group Picture:** The group picture is usually taken during the ninth week of the group. Copies of this picture can be produced and distributed to the group members during the final week. It is important to obtain permission to take a picture of each child from each caregiver; this is included as part of the GIS to be completed with the caregiver in Week 1 (See Camera with Film above).

**Handout, "How Would You Feel If":** This handout is used by the facilitators to question children about how they would feel in various situations (e.g., "How would you feel if someone broke your favorite toy?"). When the statement from the handout is read aloud, the children choose a feeling mask which indicates how they would feel in that situation. The handout can be found in Appendix 2.

**Heart Candles, Taper Candle, Matches:** Any kind of candles will work for this activity, but tea lights are often easiest. It is important to emphasize that the children can only have their candle lit when they are around an adult; and if candles are sent home, they should be accompanied by a note to the parents. Light the taper candle from the matches, and then use it to light the individual heart candles.

**Koosh® Balls:** Koosh® balls are soft plastic balls of long stringy spines. They are used in the groups for a variety of activities. The children like to hold them, especially when they are talking about things that are particularly difficult.

**Love Notes:** These are half-sheets of paper decorated with a border and called 'Love Notes.' These are notes to their special person that died. Children can tell facilitators what they would like written on the note or they can draw pictures on it. 'Love notes' can be found in Appendix 2.

**Mad Target & Wet Sponges:** The mad target is a bulls-eye style target (as used for archery) at which the wet sponges are thrown. This bulls-eye target may be made by drawing on a shower curtain using permanent markers (usually the inside circle is colored red). It is also possible to purchase prefabricated targets at sporting good stores and archery shops. If targets are purchased it is best to select waterproof versions or to laminate paper versions so they may be reused. If this activity is done inside, it is best to have a shower curtain on the floor to collect water (see Plastic Sheet below). To limit the amount of water in each sponge, cut the sponges into smaller pieces (heavy enough to throw when soaked with water, but not so large as to drench an entire wall). Don't forget a few towels to soak up the water from the shower curtain. This activity is an example of a healthy way to get out mad feelings.

**Memory Chair:** Decorate the memory chair by taping streamers to it or by draping a cloth over it. Put a sign on it designating it as The Memory Chair. It helps to have a special chair for the child to sit in while they are sharing because it cues the children to listen to the person who is sitting in the chair. It also makes the person sharing feel special.

**Memory Crown:** The memory crown can be cut out of construction paper. Decorate it with stickers, glitter, beads, or anything that makes it seem special. Make sure each child has his or her own crown to keep. Write their names on their crowns. Fasten the crowns with tape or staples, but do not fasten it until it is fitted to the child, so that each crown is the right size. A template for the memory crown can be found in Appendix 2.

**Me-sticks:** Me-sticks are used as the vehicle for the children to check-in along with the feeling face cans. Me-sticks are made out of tongue depressors and construction paper. Each child is given a different shape and color with his or her name on it. Example: red heart, yellow star, green square. Even though they may not be able to read their name, they will remember the shape and color of their Me-stick each week. The facilitators should also have a Me-stick. When the children check in, they put their Me-stick in the feeling face can that best represents how they are feeling that day. Initially, children may uniformly check in happy even though they are profoundly sad. But as the weeks progress, the children's responses will diversify as they learn how to check-in and become more honest about their feelings. They may want to put their Me-stick into more than one can, which illustrates their understanding that they can feel more than one feeling at a time.

**Name Tags:** We put name tags on the children for the first few weeks. Facilitators also wear name tags. Be certain to spell each child's name correctly and use the name he or she prefers. Sometimes, it is fun to allow children to draw or color on their name tag after you have written their names. Because the groups are limited in size, the children and facilitators usually learn each other's name after the first couple of weeks. Purchase name tags for children in an office supply or craft store, or make them.

**Picture of Cemetery and Casket:** In order to help explain the process of funerals, show the children a picture of a real cemetery and casket.

**Pictures/Belongings of Special People:** During the session on memories/remembering, children share with other group members pictures they brought and other personal belongings that remind them of their special person. Children can pass around the things that they have brought if they want, but they don't have to.

**Pictures, "What dies/What doesn't":** These are cards, about 8-1/2 x 11 inches, that have things on them that can die, such as animals (e.g., duck, cat, pig), and things that can't, such as a lamp. These may be copied onto card stock and laminated. Examples of pictures can be found in Appendix 2.

**Plastic Sheet:** Purchase a large plastic sheet to put under the sandbox, to catch the sand that spills out when the children play in it. This plastic sheet can also be used to put under the Mad Targets (above). A shower curtain may serve this purpose.

**Play-doh®:** Play-doh® is given as an option during the observed play in several sessions. In the "Identifying Changes" session, the children are encouraged to change the Play-doh® by making it into a pancake, a snake, or a donut. The facilitator can chat with the children about their own grief experiences as they work with the Play-doh

**Question Cards:** These are cards with questions printed on them that pertain to aspects around death and the child's relationship with his or her special person after the death (e.g. What reminds them of their special person?; Does anyone blame him- or herself for the death?). The children will talk about these issues with the facilitator and their peers. Put the cards in a container so that the children can pick them out of it. Question cards can be found in Appendix 2.

**Sample Notes to be Sent Home to Caregiver:** Each week a note is sent home to the caregivers. The notes let the caregivers know what the children did in group. They include reminders, when applicable, to have the child bring something the following week. For example, the note for Week 3 reminds them that the children are to bring a picture of their special person, as well as any object that reminds the children of their special person, with them the following week. The note for Week 7 reminds the children to bring a stuffed animal, or anything that comforts them, to the next session. Sample notes can be found in Appendix 3.

**Sandbox:** Use a small sandbox for the funeral of Duane—a heavy duty plastic container with a lid that can be easily stored and reused is best. Make sure that the container is deep enough to dig a hole for the casket that holds Duane. In subsequent weeks, the children can use the sandbox to perform their own burials in the observed play portion of each session. Provide them with little people figures that they can bury.

**Self-Care Bag (and self-care items):** This is a small paper bag in which several self-care items are placed. For instance, a toothbrush, hair comb, small bubble bath, shampoo, skin lotion, apple, or carrot are each items which may be placed in the bag. Each item symbolizes ways that children can take care of themselves. Each child will pick an item out of the bag and tell how he or she can use it to take care of him- or herself.

**Sheet and Nerf® Ball:** The sheet needs to be a large piece of material, such as an old bed sheet or a blanket. The size of the sheet depends on the number of children involved, but a full-sized sheet or blanket accommodates most groups. Each child should grab onto an edge of the sheet. The children will be bouncing the ball around (on the sheet), so a Nerf® ball or other soft ball should be used.

**Sheet, "Who You Gonna Call?":** This page contains a variety of statements to prompt children's responses of whom they go to for help in certain circumstances. Used in the musical chairs format, the children chant "who you gonna go to for some help, who you gonna go to for help?" as they march around empty chairs. Each child sitting in the "support" chair when the chanting is through takes a turn responding to one of the questions on the sheet. For instance, "If you fall down and get hurt, who you gonna call?" This page can be found in Appendix 2.

**Shoeboxes:** Use shoeboxes to depict various rooms in a typical home. Either wallpaper the 'walls,' paint them, or cover them with construction paper. The children can decide how many rooms their house will have. As children talk about the different changes they have experienced in the different rooms in their house since the death, they can use the small dolls to talk about it, by putting the dolls into the appropriate room.

**Snacks:**  Facilitators may decide if they wish to provide snacks each week, or just for the party on the final session. Whenever snacks are offered, be careful to check out possible food allergies with caregivers. Try to offer healthy snacks like fruit-filled breakfast bars or crackers. Individual juice drinks are handy to use for beverages. If snacks are offered each week, plan discussions around snack time.

**Stickers:**  Give the children stickers at the end of each session as a way to applaud their efforts in the group and to remind them of the group. Stickers can be symbols of various seasons or holidays such as fall or Valentine's Day. At other times stickers may go along with a theme.

**Stories, Denny the Duck Series:**  There are seven stories about a duck named Denny whose best friend, Duane, dies in a boating accident. The illustrated stories are short and correspond with the various session topics. The Denny the Duck series is written as a touchstone for the children to relate to their own stories. Each week Denny addresses a piece of his grief in the story that the children will address in the session. Two stuffed animal ducks to depict Denny and Duane that resemble the pictures in the story can be used. Ducks are fairly easy to find in the spring. When the ducks are purchased, make sure they look quite different from each other so one is not mistaken for the other.

    **"The Story of Denny the Duck":**  In this first story, the animals on the Big Pond have a funeral for Duane. After the story, the children are given an opportunity to have a funeral for Duane using the stuffed animal Duane.

    **"Life After Duane":**  This story is the second in the series of seven stories and relates to the children all of the changes that Denny experienced after Duane's death. The children have spent some time talking about the concept of change and how it surrounds us in our daily lives. This story helps the children understand how many changes we experience after a loved one dies.

    **"A Duck Never Forgets":**  This third story is about Denny missing Duane and remembering the times they spent together.

    **"A Duck has Feelings, Too":**  In this story, Denny experiences sadness, fear, anger, guilt, and happiness when thinking about Duane and Duane's death.

    **"Denny the Duck Learns About Feelings":**  Here, Denny learns that his mixed feelings about Duane's death are all part of grief. This story helps the children understand their feelings and the importance of talking about their feelings.

    **"Denny Finds Help in the Big Pond":**  Denny's friends help him by letting him know that they are his friends and that they are there for him if he needs them. This story helps children understand that there are others whom they can turn to for support.

    **"Denny Says Goodbye to Duane":**  Denny blames himself for Duane's death and realizes that death is permanent. Denny also realizes that he will always have memories of Denny in his heart.

**Superstar Medals:**  These medals may be cut out from construction paper, tagboard, or cardboard, and covered with gold colored foil. These medals are given to each child as a token denoting their participation in the grief group. Punch a hole through one of the points of the star and run string through it so that the child can wear the medal around his or her neck.

**Support Friends:** For the session "Learning Self-Care And Support," children bring with them anything that gives them comfort, such as a stuffed animal or blanket. Children keep the support friends with them, in particular during check-in and the Hokey Pokey. During the session children may share their support friends with the group. Have extra stuffed animals for any children who could not bring them.

**"Support" Sign:** Write the word "Support" on a piece of construction paper and tape it to a chair. The support chair is used for the "Who You Gonna Call?" activity, which is based on musical chairs. Whoever is sitting in the support chair when the chanting ends is asked a question from the "Who You Gonna Call?" sheet.

**Teddy Bears:** Provide teddy bears for the children to hold, if they like, during the sessions. Regulation teddy bear sized, soft, and huggable bears that are washable are best. The teddy bears are nice for the children to hold onto when the topics are particularly emotionally charged. Each week they are put out so that they are easily accessible for the children whenever they should want them.

**Tombstone:** Make a tombstone out of construction paper that can be put in the sand where Duane is buried. Write Duane's name on the tombstone. A sample tombstone can be found in Appendix 2.

**Toys:** Each session, provide some developmentally appropriate toys, such as puzzles, books, cards, play-doh, and leggos to be used by children who arrive early.

**Unfinished Business Slips on Felt Stars:** Unfinished business slips describe various things children may wish they could have done or said before the special person died (e.g. "I wish I could have said good-bye"). The descriptions may be written on small index cards and stapled to stars cut out of felt. Since preschool children cannot read, the facilitator should read the unfinished business written on the card to the children and ask the children if they have had that experience. The unfinished business slips can be found in Appendix 2.

**Wet Sponges:** See Mad Target & Wet Sponges (above).

# Samples of Materials to be Used

# CENTERING ACTIVITY OVERVIEW

Tonight we are going to take some time to do a centering. Centering means that we are going to take a trip in our imaginations. I want everyone to find a place on the floor where they can lie down. Make sure that you aren't touching anyone else. It's really important that everyone be very quiet. Instead of talking during our centering, I want you to remember the things you want to share or the answers to the questions, and we will talk about them at the end. Even if you are having a hard time imagining the trip, you still need to be very quiet and still so everyone else can do it. Okay, let's see who can be the quietest.

Close your eyes and take a quiet, deep breath in. And let it out. Breathe in. And out. Good. Now I want you to imagine a warm, soft, fluffy cloud floating gently down to you. You climb on top of the cloud and it curls up around you, so you can't fall off. Now it lifts up from the floor and it flies out the door and down the hall and outside. You can see the trees and building getting smaller and smaller as you float higher in the sky. Maybe you see a bird or two. Or maybe you see an airplane. What things can you see in the sky that you can remember to share with us later? You can smell the fresh air, and you feel very safe and peaceful on your cloud. Now it's time to turn around and to fly back to group. What sounds do you hear as you are flying? Now you can see the building and your car in the parking lot. Now you are flying lower. You fly in the door and down the hall and into the room and your cloud sets you down very gently on the floor. You know that whenever you want to feel safe and peaceful, you can call your cloud and it will float down for you. Take one last deep breath. Breathe in. And out. Whenever you are ready, you can open your eyes.

The facilitator then talks with the children about how it felt to fly on a cloud. What sorts of things did they see or hear? Where would they like to fly on their clouds next time?

## CHANGE CARDS

| | |
|---|---|
| Special person doesn't eat with me anymore | I eat less food |
| We eat different food now | No one talks at the table |
| There is an empty chair at the table now | We don't sit at the table anymore |
| I don't get tucked in anymore | I can't get to sleep |

## CHANGE CARDS

| | |
|---|---|
| I am scared of the dark now | I sleep somewhere else now |
| I have nightmares now | I don't get hugged anymore |
| My family doesn't have fun anymore | I watch more TV |
| People fight more | No one talks to each other anymore |

# CHANGE CARDS

| | |
|---|---|
| I don't get to see the person who died anymore | Sometimes I wet my pants |
| Someone else bathes me | My family doesn't play outside anymore |
| We stay home more | I have to go to a sitter now |

## CHANGE CIRCLES

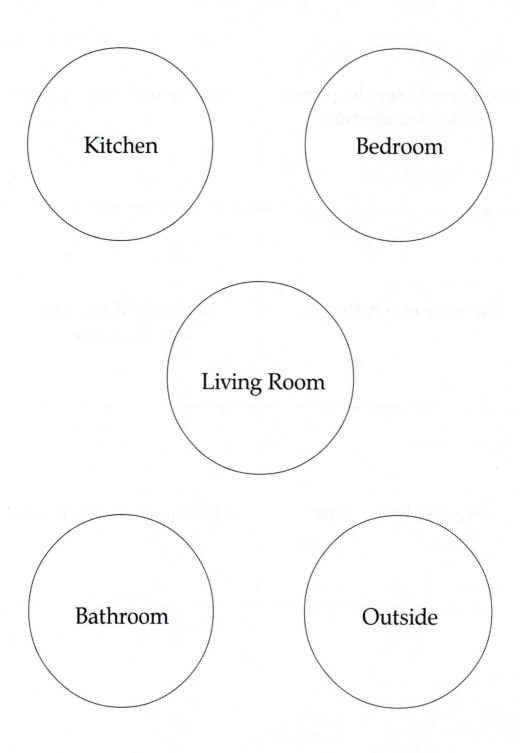

CHANGE MITTENS

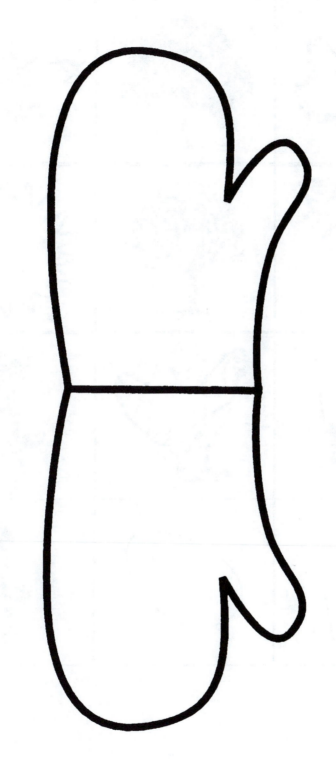

## CHANGE PICTURES

COLORING SHEET—"DENNY MISSES DUANE"

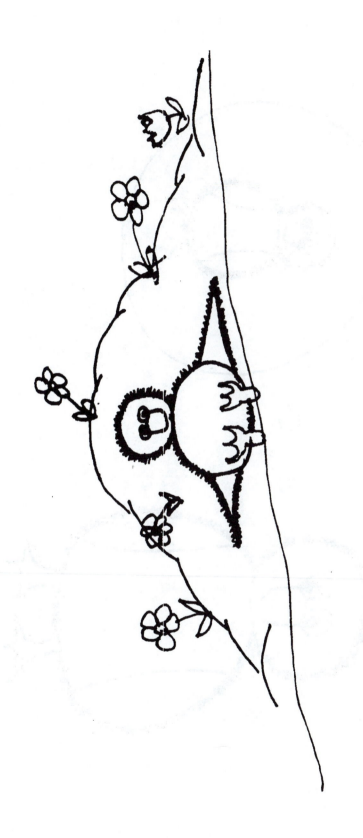

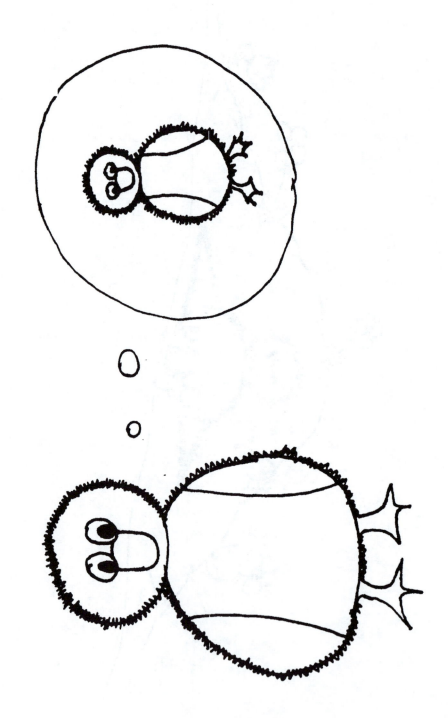

# COLORING SHEET—"DENNY THE DUCK LEARNS ABOUT FEELINGS"

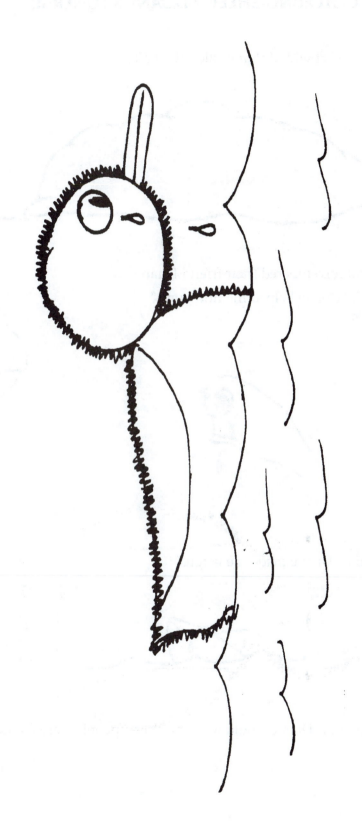

## COLORING SHEET—"DUANE'S FUNERAL"

They covered the casket with dirt and filled the hole.

Each animal friend remembered their friend Duane.
Fern the frog said, "Duane helped me find bugs."

Tom the turtle said, "Duane made me laugh."

Wally the walleye said, "Duane would warn me when people were fishing nearby."

**COLORING SHEET—"I AM FULL OF FEELINGS"**

# *I am Full of Feelings*

I am full of feelings
That are trying to get out
Sometimes when I'm feeling
I want to cry or shout
It's good to feel our feelings
It's good to get them out
Happy, sad, scared, and mad
Are what feelings are about

# COLORING SHEET—"I HAVE HELP IN MY POND OF SUPPORT"

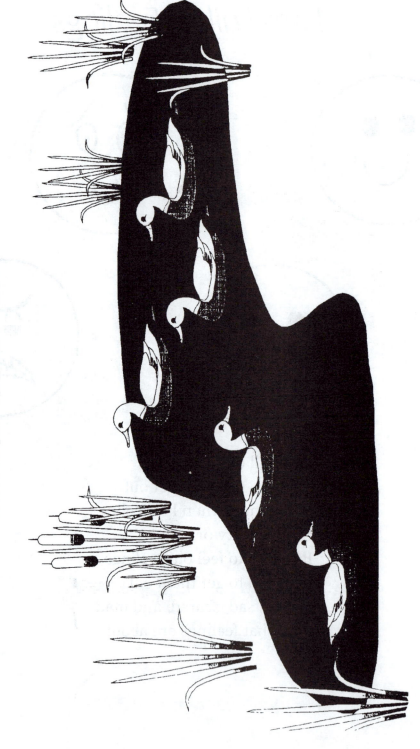

"I have help in my pond of support"

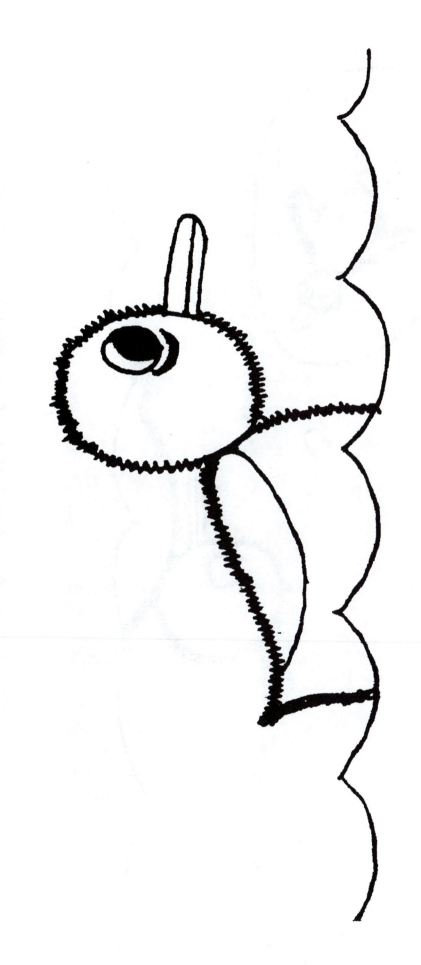

**COLORING SHEET—"LIFE AFTER DUANE" (a)**

He had a hard time sleeping at night

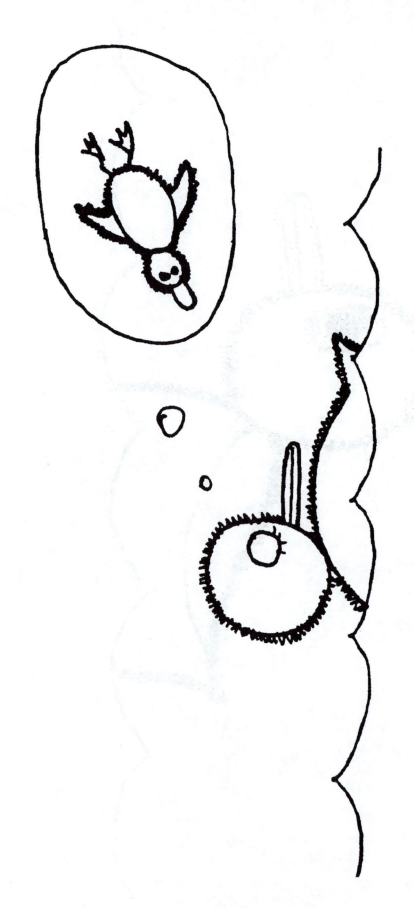

COLORING SHEET—"LIFE AFTER DUANE" (b)

and then when he did sleep, he would have nightmares and wake up screaming.

**COLORING SHEET—"LIFE AFTER DUANE"** (c)

Lots of times his tummy would hurt when he though about Duane.

## COLORING SHEET—"LIFE AFTER DUANE" (d)

He didn't feel much like doing anything because all he could do was think about Duane.

# COLORING SHEET—"SOME THINGS DIE, SOME THINGS DON'T"

## FEELING FACE CANS

**FEELING MASK—ANGRY**

# FEELING MASK—HAPPY

# FEELING MASK—SAD

## FEELING MASK—SCARED

# FLANNELBOARD BALLOON TEMPLATE

# GRIEF SUPPORT GROUPS GENERAL INFORMATION SHEET (GIS)

Child's name: _____

Today's date: _____ Date that the loss cccurred: _____

First time participant in group? Yes _____ No _____

If no, how many times has your child participated in a group

prior to the current group? _____

**Who died?**

Mother _____ Father _____ Sibling _____ Friend _____

Relative (specify) _____ Other (specify) _____

**How close was the child to the person that died?**

Not at all close _____ Somewhat close _____ Close _____ Pretty close _____

Very close _____

**What was the cause of the death?**

Illness _____ Accident _____ Sudden death (e.g., heart attack) _____

Suicide _____ Homicide ___

**Did the child witness the death?**

Yes _____ No _____

**With whom does the child currently live?**

Parent _____ (specify) Mother _____ Father _____ Sibling _____

Friend _____ Relative (specify) _____ Other (specify) _____

**Who provides the child's primary emotional support? (All that apply)**

Parent _____ Sibling _____ Friend _____ Relative (specify) _____

Mental health practitioner (specify) _____

Religious representative (e.g., nun, pastor, rabbi, priest) _____

Other (specify) _____

**What other losses has the child experienced in his or her lifetime? (All that apply)**

Death of a parent (specify) _____ Date of loss _____

Death of sibling (specify age of sibling) _____ Date of loss _____

Death of friend (specify) _____ Date of loss _____

Death of relative (specify) _____ Date of loss _____

Death of other significant person (specify) _____ Date of loss _____

Loss of home (specify) _____ Date of loss _____

Separation from sibling(s) (specify) _____ Date of loss _____

Loss of biological family unit: Foster care _____ or Adoption _____

Date of loss _____

**Had the child experienced any of the following prior to the loss? (All that apply)**

Physical abuse _____ When _____Relationship to perpetrator _____

Sexual abuse _____ When _____ Relationship to perpetrator _____

Depression _____ When _____

Suicide attempt (s) _____ When _____

Addiction/substance abuse _____ When _____

**School**

Does your child receive any special assistance at school such as tutoring, advanced placement, or special classes? (specify)

_____

_____

_____

Has the school environment been supportive of your child or have there been problems since the death? (provide details)

_____

_____

_____

**Reaction to Loss**

How does your child most easily express him- or herself (talking, writing, art, physical games)?

_____

_____

_____

What would you like the group facilitator to know about your child?

_____

_____

_____

## Relationships

How would you describe your relationship with your child? How does your child relate to other family members?

_____

_____

_____

How would you describe your child's relationship with peers (ages of peers, extrovert, introvert, leader, follower)?

_____

_____

_____

## Health

Does your child have any health concerns? Any allergies? Has he or she had any serious injuries or illnesses? Is your child taking any medications?

_____

What is your child's most frequent health problem?

_____

Will you give permission for a group picture to be taken?

Yes _____ No _____

# GLOSSARY OF FUNERAL AND DEATH TERMS

*Note:* The terms below describe specific activities or objects related to funerals and death. It's important to acknowledge that not all religions or spiritual services would include these activities or objects.

**AUTOPSY** - An autopsy is a physical examination of a dead body to find out how the person died. Not every body is given an autopsy.

**BURIAL** - The burial is the part of the funeral in which the dead body in the casket is taken to a cemetery and then buried in a hole in the ground. There may be a short religious service at the cemetery with prayers. Sometimes the casket is lowered into the ground as family and friends watch. Other times, the casket is lowered into the ground after the family leaves. The casket is lowered into a protective box in the ground called a "vault" and then covered with ground.

**CASKET** - A casket is a box that is large enough to place a dead body in it. Some caskets are plain or decorated and are made of wood. Others are made of metal. Usually when a dead body lies in the casket, only the top half of the casket is open so that the body can be seen from the waist up. When the casket is buried, it is closed and locked. Caskets are sometimes called coffins. Family members sometimes put things in the casket with the body that have special meaning. For example, the family might put something that was a belonging of the dead person such as an article of clothing.

**CEMETERY** - A cemetery is a place where dead people are buried in the ground. Usually cemeteries are large areas of land that may be surrounded by a fence. Grave markers or tombstones show where people are buried. Sometimes families and friends bring flowers to the cemetery and leave them at the grave. Sometimes, after someone dies, people visit the grave in the cemetery.

**CREMATION** - Sometimes when a person dies, the family decides to have the body cremated. When a body is cremated, it is placed in a very hot fire. The body is quickly turned into ashes. Since a dead body does not feel any pain, cremation does not hurt. After the body is cremated, it is turned into ashes. The family may choose to bury the ashes or put the ashes in a special container called an urn or spread the ashes in a special spot outdoors that means a lot to the dead person or the family.

**DEAD** - All living things die. We know that someone or something is dead when breathing stops, the heart doesn't beat, it doesn't move, it doesn't blink its eyes, it doesn't feel pain, it doesn't eat, or go to the bathroom. When someone or something dies, it cannot come back to life. In order for something or someone to die, it has to be alive first. Different living things have different life spans. That is, different living things live for different amounts of time. Most humans live to be 70-80 years old.

**DECOMPOSE** - When a person dies, his/her body decomposes. That is, the body begins to change how it looks. Eventually the body will decompose so much that all that is left is the skeletal frame of the body or the bones.

**EMBALMING** - When a person dies, the dead body is prepared for burial. This preparation is called embalming. Embalming includes removing bodily fluids and blood from the body and replacing the fluids with certain chemicals that will stop the body from decomposing too quickly.

**FUNERAL** - A funeral is a name we give to a time when we remember the person who died, look at the dead person's body, and say good-bye to the person who died. There are usually two parts to the funeral. One part is called visitation. The other part is called the burial.

**FUNERAL HOME** - A place where the dead body is taken to prepare it for burial, including placing it into a casket. Funeral homes have rooms that are used for visitations.

**GRAVE** - The place where a dead person's body is buried.

**MEMORIAL SERVICE** - A part of the funeral in which the person who died is remembered. It may or may not be a religious ceremony that would include prayers and hymns. A memorial service often includes a "eulogy" or speech that is given to remember the person who died. A eulogy might include the person's accomplishments, the name of surviving family members, qualities of that person that made him/her special or unique.

**TOMBSTONE OR HEADSTONE** - A tombstone marks the burial place of the person who died so that family and friends can find the right grave. A tombstone or headstone is placed at the "head" of the burial site or the "top" of the burial site. The tombstone is often made out of a type of stone but not always. Sometimes the grave marker is made out of wood or plastic. The tombstone will have the dead person's name on it including the year he/she was born and the year he/she died. Some tombstones may have other things engraved on them such as a Bible verse, prayer, or special saying.

**URN** - A special container that holds the ashes after a dead person has been cremated.

**VAULT** - A box that protects the casket when it is buried. When the casket is lowered into the ground, it is set into the vault in the ground.

**VISITATION** - A visitation is a time to show the dead person in the casket. A visitation can take place in a home, church, public place, or funeral home. Often family members and friends send flowers to the family in memory of the person who died. These flowers are displayed at the visitation. Most often the casket is "open." That is, the family members and friends can see the dead person lying in the casket. Sometimes family members choose to have a "closed" casket if the person who died had so many injuries or his/her body changed so much after the death, that it would be difficult to see the person that way. Family and friends come to "visit" the family and to view the dead person. That's why this part of the funeral is called a visitation. Sometimes, this part of a funeral is also called a "wake" or a "viewing."

# HANDOUT—"HOW WOULD YOU FEEL IF..."

HOW WOULD YOU FEEL IF . . . . . .

1.      You lost your caregiver in a shopping mall?

2.      Someone gave you an ice cream cone?

3.      Your best friend moved away?

4.      You went to the cemetery and visited the grave of your special person?

5.      Someone broke your favorite toy?

6.      Someone pushed you down on the playground?

7.      You got to go to the zoo?

8.      You got a new bike?

9.      You watched a scary show on TV?

10.     Your brother or sister kept teasing you?

11.     You saw your caregiver cry because of the death of your special person?

12.     Your caregiver got sick and couldn't get out of bed?

13.     You got in a car accident?

14.     Your pet didn't come home one day when it got out?

15.     Your caregiver wouldn't let you watch TV?

16.     Your caregiver sent you to your room?

17.     There was a bad storm with lots of thunder and lightning?

18.     Your caregiver made you eat spinach?

❤ *L O V E   N O T E S* ❤

❤ *L O V E   N O T E S* ❤

MEMORY CROWN

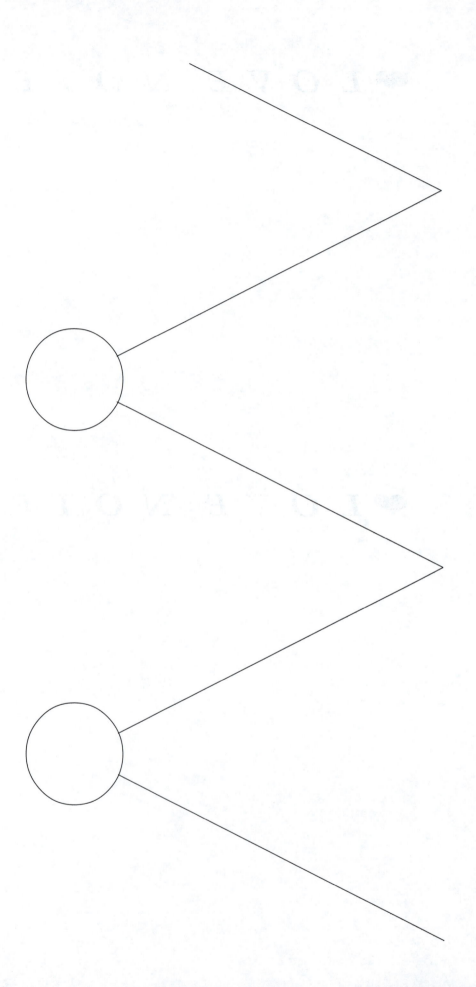

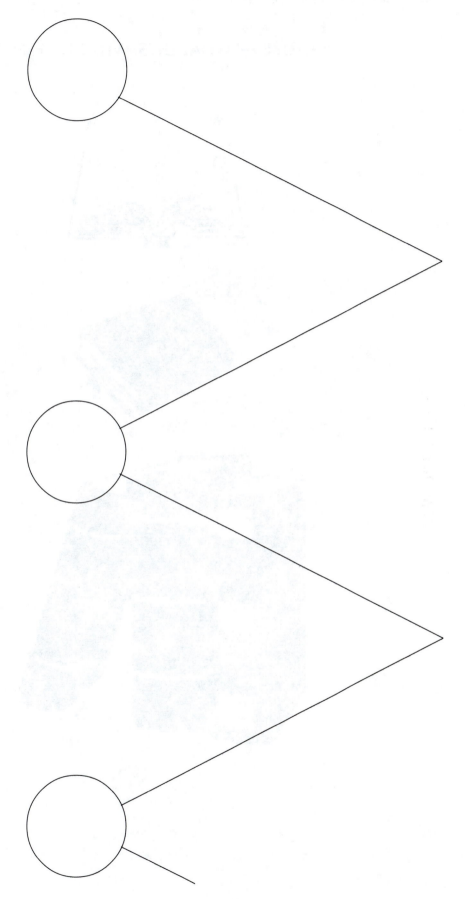

# PICTURES—"WHAT DIES/WHAT DOESN'T"

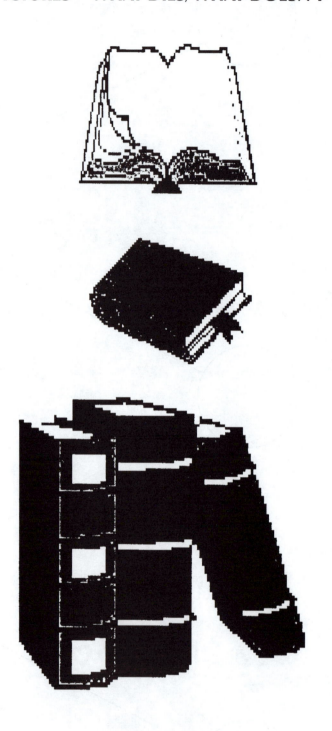

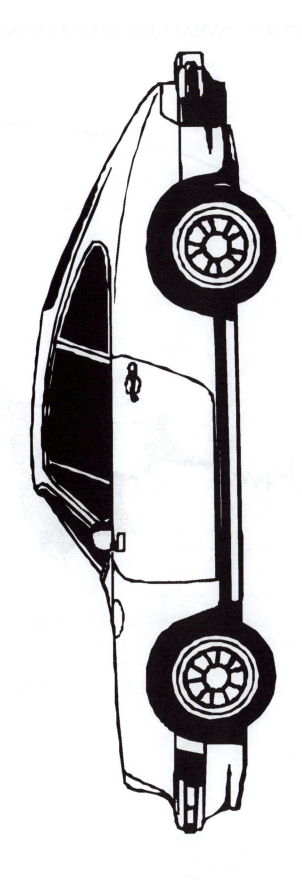

# PICTURES—"WHAT DIES/WHAT DOESN'T"

# PICTURES—"WHAT DIES/WHAT DOESN'T"

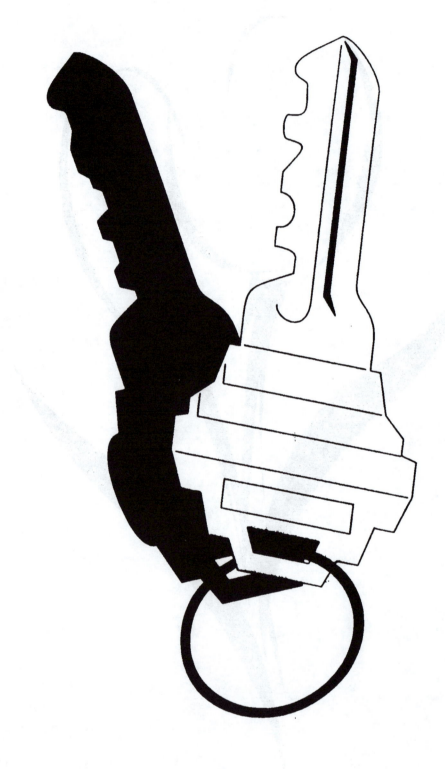

# PICTURES—"WHAT DIES/WHAT DOESN'T"

## PICTURES—"WHAT DIES/WHAT DOESN'T"

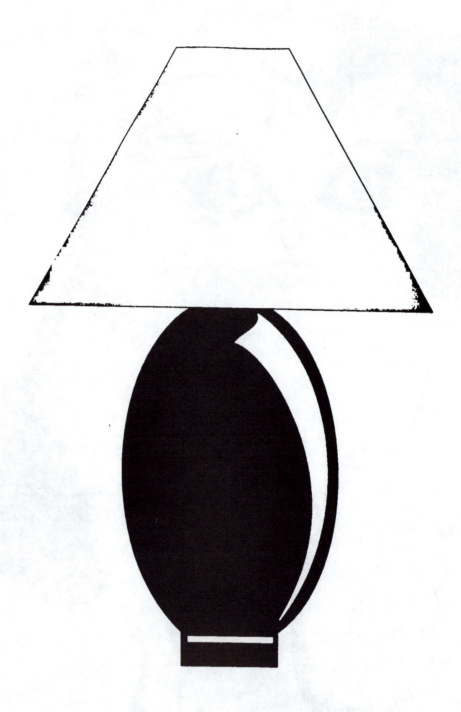

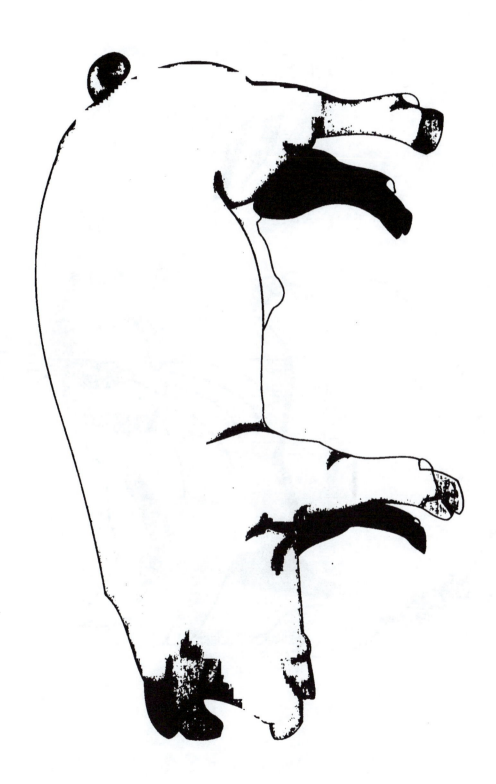

PICTURES—"WHAT DIES/WHAT DOESN'T"

## PICTURES—"WHAT DIES/WHAT DOESN'T"

PICTURES—"WHAT DIES/WHAT DOESN'T"

## PICTURES—"WHAT DIES/WHAT DOESN'T"

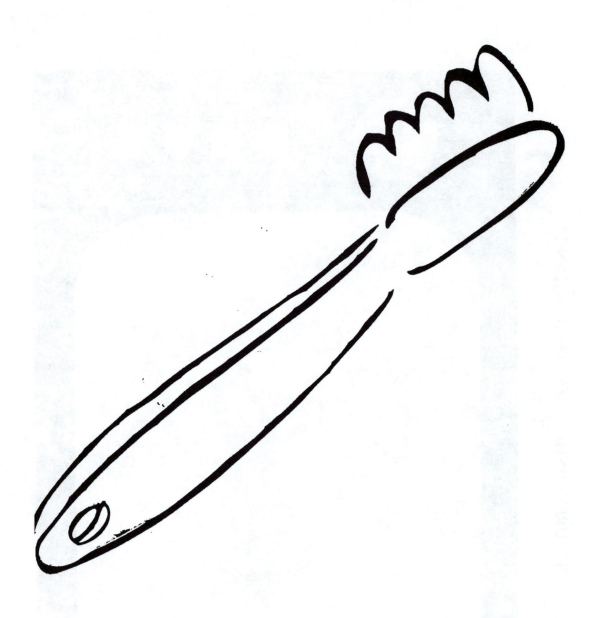

## PICTURES—"WHAT DIES/WHAT DOESN'T"

## QUESTION CARDS

| | |
|---|---|
| How did your body feel when you found out your special person died? | Who helped you on the days around the funeral? |
| What time of day did your special person die? | Did you go to the funeral? |
| Did you get to see the body? If you did, what was it like seeing the body? If you did not get to see the body, what was that like? | Did you get to say good-bye to your special person who died? |

## QUESTION CARDS

| | |
|---|---|
| Did you participate in the funeral? | What do you remember about the funeral? |
| What do you remember about the cemetery? | Are there any questions you have about the death of your special person that no one has answered for you? |
| Where do you think your special person is now? | What do you remember about the last time you saw your special person alive? |

## QUESTION CARDS

| | |
|---|---|
| After your special person died, what is something that someone said to you that you thought was helpful? | After your special person died, what is something that someone said to you that you thought was stupid? |
| Did you know that your special person was going to die? | Was your special person's body buried in the ground or was it cremated? What do you remember about this ? |
| Were you with your special person when he/she died? Tell us about that. | Who told you about the death of your special person and what did they tell you? |

## QUESTION CARDS

| | |
|---|---|
| What do you remember about when your special person died? | Did you go to the funeral? Tell us about that. |
| Did you get to see the body of your special person who died? Tell us about that. | |

# SHEET—"WHO YOU GONNA CALL?"

## Who You Gonna Call IF . . .

1. You want to play?

2. You need someone to fix a toy, bike?

3. You need a hug?

4. You feel sad about your special person that died?

5. You need to talk about your special person that died?

6. You have questions about the death of your special person or things that you don't understand?

7. You need to get away from the house to play?

8. You feel angry at a brother, sister, or friend?

9. You are having trouble sleeping at night?

10. You feel guilty about something?

11. You have something to talk about that is hard to talk about?

12. You are having problems with your caregiver?

13. There is a fire in your house and your caregivers aren't home?

14. You have questions about God or heaven?

15. You are afraid that you might die?

# SUPERSTAR MEDALS

## TOMBSTONE

DUANE
THE
DUCK

# UNFINISHED BUSINESS SLIPS ON FELT STARS

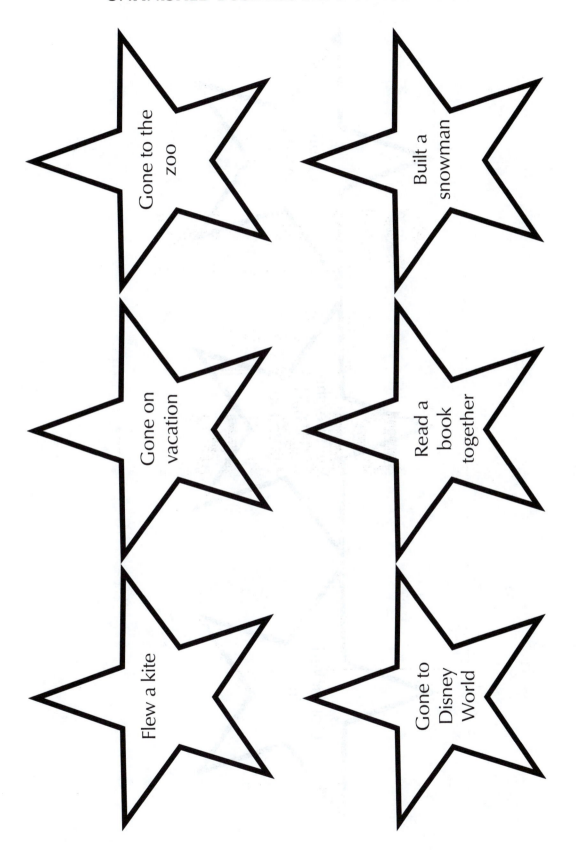

## UNFINISHED BUSINESS SLIPS ON FELT STARS

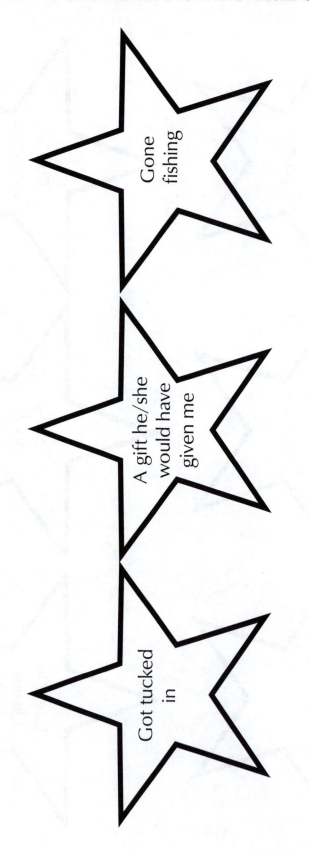

# Sample Notes to be Sent Home to Caregivers

■ **Week 2: Telling My Story**

"I like me . . . I like me . . . ;" that's how we started our group today. We will start our group with this song each week. Ask me to sing it for you. After we sang our song, we got to know each other by throwing a Koosh® ball to each other and saying something about ourselves. Then we looked at a flannelboard and counted the balloons on it. There were 9 balloons on it. We removed one. That means we have 8 more weeks left. Tonight we learned what a check-in is. A check-in is a time when we share with each other how we are feeling. Then we met Chuck the Feeling Doll. Each week we will check in with Chuck to see how he is feeling. Tonight Chuck was feeling happy. Then we each told each other who died, and how they died. Ask me about it. After that we took a break to get the wiggles out and sang, "Head, Shoulders, Knees, and Toes." Then we talked about what 'dead' means. We learned that when something is dead, it doesn't breathe, its heart doesn't beat, and it doesn't sleep, grow, blink its eyes, or feel any pain. We looked at some dead things and talked about how we knew these things were dead. Then we looked at some pictures of things and had to say whether they can die or not. We learned that all living things die. Then we had some observed play. We could color a coloring sheet, or play with a puzzle or Play-doh®. We ended our group with our song.

## ■ Week 3: Exploring Death

We started our group with our song again and then we had a centering activity. A centering activity is a time that we spend quieting down from the day and getting ourselves ready for group. Then we had a check-in. Chuck the Feeling Doll checked in, too. Then we took another balloon from the flannelboard. We have 7 more weeks left. After that we reviewed what we learned about the word 'dead' last week. Then we met Denny the Duck and heard a story about Denny and his friend Duane. Duane died after a boat hit him. Then we had a funeral for Duane. We dug a hole and put his casket in it. We learned many funeral terms. Ask me about Duane's funeral. Each week we will have a story about Denny and his experience after the death of Duane. After Duane's funeral we had observed play. We could color or play in the sandbox. The most important thing we learned today was that when someone dies, we need to keep asking questions to someone we can trust. We need to get our questions answered.

## ■ Week 4: Identifying Changes

We began our group with our song again and then had a centering activity. After that we had a check-in. Chuck checked in scared tonight. Then we removed another balloon from the flannelboard. We have 6 more weeks left. After that we talked about change. We learned that change means that something is different. We talked about things that change around us everyday. We talked about things that we can make change (like changing our clothes) and things we can't make change (like the weather, it just happens). We talked about how when a special person dies, there can be lots of changes. These are changes we did not create. Then we looked for pictures of changes hidden around the room. Once we found all of the pictures we matched up the changes (like matching an egg with a chicken, or day with night). We learned that there are lots of changes around us everyday. After that we read another story about Denny the Duck called "Life after Duane." The story told us about all of the changes Denny experienced after Duane died. Then we took a break. We pretended to be baby kangaroos climbing out of our mothers' pouches and hopping around the room. Then we pretended to be a kernel of popcorn popping in a popcorn popper. That was fun! After that we played a modified version of "London Bridge" and sang a song called "Life is changing all around." Ask me to sing it for you. Whoever got caught in the bridge picked a circle from a bag. Each circle represented a room in the house. Our facilitator read what was on the corresponding card and we had to say whether we had experienced that change since our special person died. We learned that we have had lots of changes since our special person died. After that we had observed play. We could color a coloring sheet or play with the playhouse rooms and people. We ended our group with our song.

*Caregiver:* Next week your child should bring a picture of his or her special person to group as well as something that reminds him or her of that person.

## ■ Week 5: Memories/Remembering

We began our group with our song again and then a centering activity. Then we had a check-in. Tonight Chuck the Feeling Doll was feeling sad. Then we removed one more balloon from the flannelboard. We have 5 more weeks left. After that we talked about memories. We learned that memories are like walking backwards in your mind. Then we spent some time sharing the pictures and belongings of our special person that we brought to group. We got to sit in a special memory chair and we each got a memory crown to wear. Then we had a break. We had to keep a Nerf® ball on a sheet as we moved it up and down. That was fun! After that we read another story about Denny the Duck. Tonight's story was about all of the memories that Denny has of his friend Duane. Then we looked at something called a Forget-Me-Not tray. It had lots of different things on it. We had to close our eyes and then something was removed from the tray. We had to say what was missing. The Forget-Me-Not tray reminds us that even though our special person is no longer with us, we will always remember that they were here with us and still are here in our memories. Then we had observed play. After that we each got a candle and lit it in memory of our special person. We ended our group with our song.

*Caregiver:* Tonight your child is bringing home a candle to burn in memory of his or her special person. We urge you to caution your child only to burn the candle in the presence of an adult.

## ■ Week 6: Identifying and Expressing Feelings

We began our group with our song again. Then we had a centering activity. After that we took one more balloon from the flannelboard. We have 4 more weeks left. Then we had a check-in. Tonight Chuck the Feeling Doll was feeling mad. Then we talked about feelings. We blew bubbles and talked about how bubbles are like feelings. Some bubbles were big, some were small; some bubbles popped quickly, others stayed for a while. No two bubbles were alike. That's how feelings are. Some feelings are big, others are small. Some feelings come and go quickly, others stay. No two feelings are the same. We learned that when a special person dies, we can have lots of different feelings and it's okay to have feelings. Then we did a movement activity. After that we read another story about Denny the Duck called "A Duck Has Feelings Too!" Then we sang "When You're Happy and You Know It." Then we used masks with different feelings on them. We had to hold up the mask that showed how we might feel if a certain thing happened to us (e.g. "how would you feel if someone broke your favorite toy."). After that we had observed play. Then we ended our group with our song.

## ■ Week 7: Exploring Unfinished Business

We started our group with our song again and then did a centering activity. Then we had a check-in. After that we took another balloon from the flannelboard. We have 3 more weeks left. Then we talked about our topic: unfinished business. We learned that sometimes when a special person dies, we don't get to say good-bye to them. Sometimes there are things we don't get to do with that person, and there are things we don't get to do with them anymore. Those are the things we talked about tonight. We read another story about Denny the Duck called "I Didn't Get to Say Good-bye" to help us talk about the topic. After that we took a break. Then we played a game exploring questions. After that we each wrote a love note to our special person. We learned that even though our special person has died, we can still talk to him or her and remember him or her. Then we had observed play. We ended our group with our song.

*Caregiver:* The children spent some time writing a love note to their special people tonight. We encourage you to spend some time with your child talking to him or her about what he or she would like to do with the note. Does your child want to take it to the cemetery? Keep it in a special place? Burn it? (in your presence, of course). These love notes are intended to encourage the children to communicate with their special people. Talking with your child about the love note affords you the opportunity to talk with your child about the death of the special person.

## ■ Week 8: Coping With Feelings

We began our group with our song again. Then we had a centering activity. After that we had a check-in. Tonight Chuck was feeling scared. After that we took another balloon from the flannelboard. We have 2 more weeks left. Then we talked about what can happen to our feelings if we don't get them out. We used a balloon to show what can happen. If we keep blowing air into the balloon, eventually it will pop and break. That's what can happen to us if we don't get our feelings out. They will get bigger and bigger until we can't hold them in anymore and our feelings will pop out. Then we pretended to be balloons and took in lots of air. Then we let the air out, and that felt much better. That's how it is if we let our feelings out. We feel so much better. After that we read another story about Denny the Duck. Denny learned about feelings from his friend Tom the Turtle. Ask me about the story. Then we had a break and sang a song called "POP! Go My Feelings!" sung to the tune of "POP! Goes the Weasel." Then we threw wet sponges at a mad target to help us express our anger. After that we had observed play. We ended our group with our song.

*Caregiver:* Next week the children are going to talk about support. They should bring their favorite stuffed animal or blanket to group with them. Also, next week there will be a group picture taken. Your child will get a copy of the picture to take home with him/her on the last night of group.

## ■ Week 9: Learning about Self-Care and Support

We began our group with our song again and had a centering activity. Then we had our check-in. We each showed what support friends we brought with us tonight. We checked in with Chuck to see how he was feeling. Then we removed another balloon from the flannelboard. We have one more week left. Then we talked about self-care and found out that self-care means taking care of ourselves. We also talked about support. We learned that support means "help." We illustrated what support is by building a tower with blocks. We found out that if the tower doesn't have enough support, it will fall down. But if the tower does, it will stand straight and tall. That's how it is when we do or do not have enough support after a special person dies. Then we took a break and danced the Hokey-Pokey with our special support friends. That was fun! Then we played a game like musical chairs about support, where we talked about who we could go to for support in different situations. Ask me about it. Then we read another story about Denny the Duck where Denny learned about support. After that we looked in a paper bag that had items for self-care in them. We had to think about how we could use each object to take care of ourselves. Then we had observed play. We ended our group with our song again.

*Caregiver:* Next week is the last night of group. There will be a closing ceremony after group to remember the special person. You are invited. Refreshments will be served after the ceremony.

## ■ Week 10: Learning to Say Good-Bye

We started our group with our song and then had a centering activity. After that we had a check-in. Chuck the Feeling Doll said good-bye to all of us. Then we removed the last balloon from the flannelboard. We have no more weeks left of group. Then we each got Superstar medals for all of the good work we have done in the group. Then we read the Denny the Duck story from beginning to end. Then we each got a Denny the Duck. After that we had a small party. Then we sang our song for the last time.

# Special Activities: Holidays

**Valentine's Day:** An activity that can be fun for children on Valentine's Day is to bring heart-shaped cookies and a tub of frosting and let the children decorate their own cookies.

**Mother's Day and Father's Day:** If a child has had a parent die, both holidays are difficult. The parent who died may have helped in planning the celebrations and in buying or making gifts. For example, if the mother died, the child may not have the resources to make a Father's Day gift. The day serves a heightened reminder of the loss. In other words, children are acutely aware of the loss of their father on Father's Day. In group, it is important to talk about the holiday during check-in and ask people what they are feeling about it. It may also be appropriate to make a gift during group. It can help the child to talk about how even though the parent died, he or she is still the child's parent and the child might want to remember their parent with a gift that can be left at the grave or kept someplace special.

**Independence Day:** Fireworks are often the most exciting part of the Fourth of July for kids. Use fireworks to talk about the feelings they have. Ask them how fireworks are like feelings. Fireworks change color; some are loud and scary; some make us happy; some fireworks last a long time; sometimes they are duds. Have them color a picture of what sets off their feeling fireworks.

**Halloween:** Halloween is a good opportunity to talk about the scary myths about death in popular culture. Gather some Halloween decorations such as skeletons and mummies and talk about what they mean. It is also a good time to talk about what children can do to take care of themselves when they feel afraid. Tailor an activity around trick-or-treating. Have a gift bag or a fake jack-o-lantern. Fill it with slips of paper. On one side of each paper, draw candy such as Snickers®, M&Ms®, and Twix®. On the other side, write a question. This activity can work for many topics.

**Thanksgiving:** Because families gather together at this time, many feelings may resurface for the children because of the absence of their special person. These aspects of the holiday should be discussed in group. The group may also discuss "giving thanks" for living family members or for the special memories they have of their special person.

**Christmas/Hanukkah/Kwanzaa:** These holidays may evoke the same feelings as does Thanksgiving. It can be helpful to talk with children about special holiday traditions they shared with their special person. How can they remember their special person during this time? Maybe they want to continue a tradition that they used to share with their special person or maybe they want to do something different. Help the children find ways to talk with their family about what they are feeling and what would be helpful to them during the holidays.

**Birthdays:** Celebrating birthdays in a time-limited group is hard because not everyone's birthday falls during the session. Those children whose birthdays are at other times of the year may feel left out. Birthdays can be acknowledged during check-in and it can be an opportunity to talk about how birthdays feel when our loved ones have died. If the children really want to celebrate, have an Unbirthday Party for everyone in the group. Wrap little gift boxes with questions in them that pertain to the gifts received from the person who died. Questions could include: what is something special my special person gave me?; what is a quality that I share with my special person?; what did my special person teach me that I always want to remember?

# Sample Curriculum
# for a Special Day

## ■ Holiday Heartaches

This session is intended for use when a holiday falls during the week of the group meeting. These holiday themes can be incorporated into the grief curriculum to help the children through the holidays, which can be especially difficult times. Activities during this session may be incorporated into any of the sessions. The children can visit towns on their griefmobiles that coincide with the particular holiday, and share feelings surrounding this experience. They can also make gifts for their special people, for example, Christmas/Hanukkah/Kwanzaa presents to help remember their special people and to share the holiday with them. The holiday session is important given that during these times, issues surrounding the loss are especially salient.

## Objectives

> To remember the child's special person from holidays past
> To remember holidays from the past
> To identify how holidays are different now
> To talk about ways to remember the child's special person during the holidays

## Materials

Chuck, the Feeling Doll  
Crayons  
Feeling face cans  
Gift bag  
Gift boxes  
Holiday gifts  
Holiday items  

Memory sheet  
Me-sticks  
Remembrance candles  
Gold elastic string  
Large translucent beads (red, white, clear)  
Pipecleaners  
Ribbon to match

## Procedures

*Note:* A star (\*) by an activity denotes that this is a main activity, considered central to the session. Unstarred activities are supplemental activities.

### *Opening Activity\**

Use the same procedures outlined in Week 2.

### *Centering Activity\**

**Materials**
    Centering activity overview
    (See Appendix 2 for centering activity overview)

Use the same procedures outlined in Week 3.

### *Sharing Feelings (Check-In)\**

**Materials**
    Chuck the Feeling Doll

After the children see how Chuck is feeling about the holidays, ask the following questions: "What are you dreading about the holidays? What are you looking forward to? What will you do the same? What will you do different? Is it okay to be happy and excited about the holidays? How will you remember your loved one over the holidays? Is there some way you can memorialize them?"

### *Introduction To The Topic: Holiday Heartaches\**

**Materials**
    Christmas, Kwanzaa, Hanukkah Items

"Tonight we are going to talk about the holidays that we will be celebrating in a short while. Does anyone know what a holiday is? A holiday is a day of special celebration in which families get together and carry out certain things that they do year after year. Can anyone name what those holidays might be? (Christmas? Kwanzaa? Hanukah?) When a special person dies, we really miss them around the holiday season and our holiday may be different from other years. We remember your special person who died, and we remember holidays that we spent with them in the past. Let's see if we can recall certain memories about the upcoming holidays." Give each one of the children an item from the holiday. Have some symbols from Christmas, Kwanzaa, and Hanukkah.

Examples of things to bring are:

| | |
|---|---|
| Angels | Kwanzaa candles |
| Bells | Menorah |
| Candy canes | Reindeer |
| Christmas lights | Santa |
| Christmas tree decorations | Snowmen |
| Christmas wreath | Tree |
| Dreidel | Wrapping paper |

Pass out one of these things to each of the children. Children then take turns talking about the item that they have and if they have any memories of this item. Remind the children that these things are holiday reminders and when they celebrate the holidays this year the items will also remind us of the children's special person who died because that person is no longer with them to celebrate the holidays. Children are encouraged to recall any memories they have of that item with their special person.

## Gifts From Our Special People

**Materials**
    Gift bag
    Gift boxes
    Memory sheet
    (See last page of this Appendix for memory sheet)

Explain "When we celebrate holidays this time of year, we often give gifts to each other. Tonight we are going to open up our very special gifts to share with each other. These gifts are not toys or things we can play with, but rather are gifts our special person gave us in the form of a memory. We will each take turns picking a gift from the pouch (any small bag that will hold the gift boxes). Inside of the gift box you will find a very special memory that your special person who died has given to you in the form of a memory (the gift boxes can be small jewelry boxes that have the message inside). Remember what a memory is?" Each child then opens his or her gift and talks about what memory he or she has that is printed on the slip of paper inside. Explain that even though the child's special person cannot be with him or her this year, the special person has given the child a very special gift in the form of a memory that can always be kept.

## Take 5

Fun activity of choice.

## Remembrance (Tree) Ornament or Sun-Catcher

**Materials**
Gold elastic string
Large translucent beads (red, white, clear)
Pipecleaners
Ribbon to match

Explain, "Now we are going to remember your special person who died by making something in memory of your special person. You can choose to make a tree ornament or a sun-catcher to hang in your window at home. Decide what shape you want your ornament or sun-catcher to be. Suggestions are a heart or star. Now thread your beads through the pipe cleaner until you have enough to shape it."

## Closing*

Use the same procedures outlined in Week 2.

## A Reminder

**Materials**
Stickers

Use the same procedures outlined in Week 2.

## MEMORY SHEET

Remember a gift he/she gave you
Remember a gift you gave him/her
Remember your holiday last year
Remember a holiday when your special person was alive
If your special person was here with you this year, what gift would she/he give you?
Something you did with your special person around the holidays
A TV show that you watched together around the holidays
A holiday movie that you watched with your special person
Remember something you did on New Year's Eve
Remember decorating the tree with your special person
Remember something funny around the holiday
Remember a holiday meal you ate with your special person

# Denny the Duck Stories

# The Story of Denny the Duck

*by Linda Lehmann*
*illustrated by John Norquist*
*edited by Shane R. Jimerson*

This is a story about Denny the duck. Denny lived in the Big Pond in the northland with many animal friends. His best friend was Duane the duck. Denny and Duane played together every day, all day long. Whenever you saw Denny, Duane was not far away.

One day Denny and Duane decided to go for a swim in a nearby lake. They liked the lake because it had clear water and delicious plants to eat. Lately though, the lake was full of boats and that made it hard to swim.

Duane was showing off his triple somersault when something happened. All of a sudden, a boat came out of nowhere and . . . POW!

Duane got hit and he flew through the air. He landed on the shore. Denny quickly swam to the shore where Denny lay. He wasn't moving. Denny called Duane, "Duane! Duane!" But Duane did not move. Duane was dead.

Denny listened to Duane's heart and it wasn't beating. He wasn't breathing either. When Denny touched Duane he didn't move. Duane didn't hear Denny when he called his name.

Soon other animal friends came from all around. Tom the turtle stepped forward and spoke, "Denny, Duane is dead. The boat hit him too hard and he got hurt too much. His body died. We must have a funeral for him." "But it was my fault!" said Denny, "I shouldn't have brought Denny here to swim."

"It's no one's fault Denny," said Tom. "You didn't see the boat and the boat didn't see you and Duane. It was an accident. Come, let's go find a box to put Duane's body in so we can bury him." The animal friends dug a hole to put Duane's casket in. They put his body in the casket and put it in the ground.

They covered the casket with dirt and filled the hole.

Each animal friend remembered their friend Duane.

Fern the frog said, "Duane helped me find bugs."

Tom the turtle said, "Duane made me laugh."

Wally the walleye said, "Duane would warn me when people were fishing nearby."

And finally Denny said, "He was my best friend . . . I will never forget him . . . I will miss him."

The animals planted wild flowers on top of the grave where Duane was buried.  The animals in the Big Pond never forgot their friend Duane the duck.  In fact, if you go there, you will find wildflowers along the shore where Duane's body is buried.  The beautiful flowers remind all of the animals in the Big Pond of their friend, Duane the duck.

THE END

# Life After Duane

*by Linda Lehmann*
*illustrated by John Norquist*
*edited by Shane R. Jimerson*

After Duane died, life seemed so different for Denny. Everything was different, nothing seemed the same. Everything had "changed" . . .

He had a hard time sleeping at night

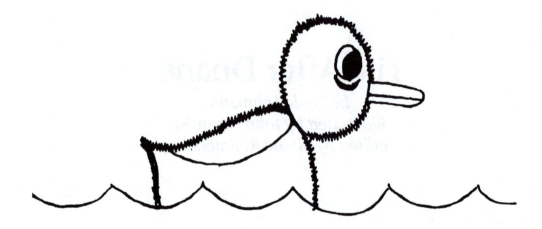

and then when he did sleep, he would have nightmares and wake up screaming.

Lots of times his tummy would hurt when he thought about Duane.

He didn't feel much like doing anything because all he could do was think about Duane.

Life was so different, Denny wondered whether things would ever be the same again. Tom the turtle saw Denny sitting by himself. "What's the matter Denny?" asked Tom.

"Oh, I was just thinking about how things have changed since Duane died. The Big Pond has changed; I have changed. Will things ever be the same as they were before?"

"Well, Denny, some things will never be the same because Duane is dead and that won't change. But some things won't always be this way. The hardest thing when someone dies is 'change.' We just need to ask our friends to help us by letting us talk about the changes, and let them give us help if we need it." "Thanks, Tom. It did help to talk." "Any time, Denny any time."

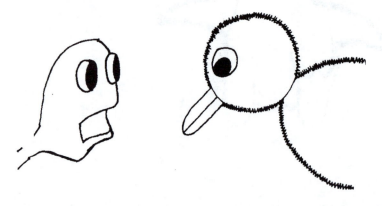

## THE END

# A Duck Never Forgets

by Linda Lehmann
illustrated by John Norquist
edited by Shane R. Jimerson

One day not long after Duane died, Denny was sitting all alone by Duane's grave thinking about his friend who died. He missed Duane so much. He would think about Duane all the time and remember him because a duck never forgets.

He remembered how Duane swam through the water. He was the best swimmer in the pond. He could swim faster and further than anyone and for miles around.

He remembered how Duane would make him laugh with all of the many tricks he would play on the other animals. He would laugh out loud when he remembered how Duane would come up under a lily pad that Fern the frog was sitting on and scare her.

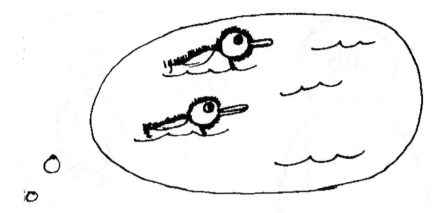

He remembered how he and Duane would visit nearby lakes and swim together for hours laughing and giggling all the way.

He loved how Duane would swoop down in the lake and say, "Hey Denny, do you want to go play?"

Denny missed all of those things about Duane. Those things are called memories. Memories were all that Denny had left. They helped Denny remember Duane. He knew that even though Duane was dead, he would never forget him because a duck never forgets important things and Duane was the most important friend a duck could ever have.

THE END

# A Duck Has Feelings Too

by Linda Lehmann
illustrated by John Norquist
edited by Shane R. Jimerson

After Duane died, Denny had lots of feelings. Sometimes he would think about Duane and be very SAD. He would cry and cry. He cried so much he thought he would cry a lake of tears.

Sometimes when he thought about how Duane died, he got SCARED. He worried that he might die too! When he felt scared he would suck on his foot and shake all over.

Sometimes when he thought about the boat that hit Duane and killed him, he would feel MAD!! He would throw seaweed at the shore and splash the water as he pounded it with his wing!

Sometimes when he thought about Duane he would wonder if Duane's death was his fault. After all, he was the one who suggested they go swimming that day. When he felt GUILTY he would hide his head under his wing.

Sometimes when he would remember the fun times he had with Duane he would smile and feel HAPPY.

But sometimes he would feel all of these feelings all at once and he didn't know what he was feeling. All of these together are called "grief." When someone we love dies, we have lots of feelings. The feelings we have when someone dies are called "grief." All of these feelings are okay to have. The important thing is to tell someone and talk about what you are feeling.

THE END

# Denny Says Good-Bye to Duane

*by Linda Lehmann*
*illustrated by John Norquist*
*edited by Shane R. Jimerson*

One day Denny was swimming in the big pond and thinking about his friend Duane who died. You see Duane was hit by a boat and died. He swam by the spot where Duane got hit and remembered that terrible moment.

Denny started to cry. "If only I would have seen the boat coming! Maybe it's my fault Duane died. I shouldn't have let him do that somersault. I should have protected Duane."

"Well, you always make me laugh," said Denny. "Everyone needs someone to have fun with," said Wally, "I like to make you laugh." Wally heard some fishing boats nearby and decided he better go. "See you soon Denny," he said, "Gotta go!" Denny watched Wally swim away and thought, "Everyone should have someone to have fun with." Then he heard someone croaking a song on a nearby lily pad.

It was Fern the frog waiting for an occasional fly to come her way. "Hi, Denny," said Fern, "How are you today?" "Oh, I'm all right," said Denny, "Except that I miss Duane and I don't feel like I have any friends." "No friends?" said Fern, "Why nobody has more friends in the Big Pond than you Denny. It's just that sometimes we don't know how to help you since Duane died."

"Right," said Denny. "How could you, just a little duck, have stopped that big boat?" said Tom. "Well, I don't know," said Denny. "Don't you think it is time to quit blaming yourself Denny?" questioned Tom. Denny answered, "Well, I guess you are right." "Of course I am. Now if you'll excuse me, I was taking a nap."

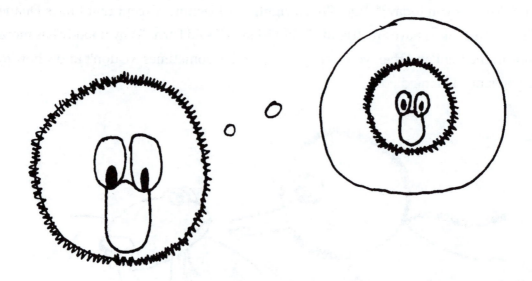

"Okay," said Denny and he swam away. But all day long Denny could only think about his friend Duane. They had so many things they were going to do together and now they wouldn't be able to.

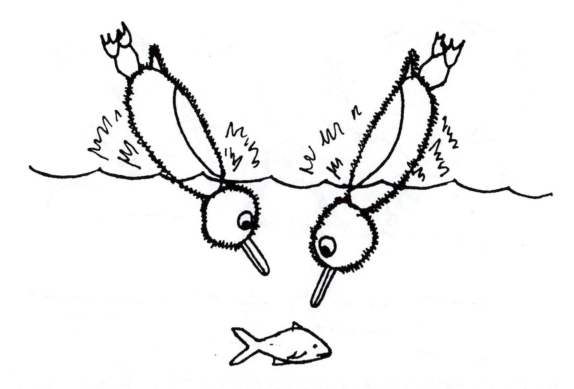

Before Duane died, they had planned to take a trip to Canada to do some fishing. Now they wouldn't be able to go. And they were going to be the biggest, strongest ducks on the pond. They would fish the best, swim the best, and fly the furthest. And now there was just Denny to fish alone, to swim alone, and to fly alone. Denny learned that's what happens when someone dies, there are so many things you can't do with them anymore.

It was sundown by the time Denny reached the shore by Duane's grave. He started to talk, "I never got to say good-bye. I miss you Duane. I miss you so much. You were my best friend and I will never forget you. I feel better when I come to your grave and visit you. I guess I'll always be able to do that. Even though I didn't get to say good-bye I know that I can talk to you anytime I want to."

Denny swam home that night feeling better.
He knew that Duane was never far away
because he would always remember him
and he would remain in his heart forever.

THE END

# Denny the Duck Learns About Feelings

*by Linda Lehmann*
*illustrated by John Norquist*
*edited by Shane R. Jimerson*

One day Denny the duck was floating around in the water and something wasn't just right. He had lots of different mixed up feelings. He felt happy, sad, scared, and mad all at once. He was just not feeling right and was really crabby. He said to himself, "I just don't know what's wrong with me. There's no reason for me to be feeling this way."

Suddenly, Wally the walleye popped up out of the water and yelled, "Boo!" behind Denny. Denny jumped three feet off of the water. When he turned around to see that Wally was playing a trick on him, he got really mad. "Hey," he screamed, "What are you doing?" Wally laughed, "Oh, I was just playing around." "Oh yeah!" screamed Denny, "Go play somewhere else. I'm not in the mood for your silliness!" "All right, all right," said Wally, "Don't ruffle your feathers!" And with that, Wally went away under water.

"Who does he think he is bothering me like that?" thought Denny. He continued to swim around. Then Denny ran into Fern the frog sitting on a lily pad. She was waiting for a fly to come by so she could have lunch. "Hi Denny," said Fern. And Denny just kept on swimming by. "Denny, Hello!..." But Denny didn't hear Fern call out to him. "I wonder what is wrong with Denny," thought Fern, "He looks like he is not doing too good."

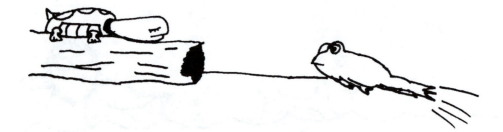

Just then she spotted Tom the turtle taking a nap over on a log nearby. She hippity hopped over to him and woke him up gently. "Tom, Tom, wake up! I've got to talk to you about something." Tom opened his eyes very slowly. "Hi Fern," he yawned, "What can I do for you?" Fern said, "Have you seen Denny today? He doesn't look like he's doing very well. I wonder what's wrong." "What's wrong? What's wrong?" Tom said, "I think I know what's wrong. He's grieving Duane. He misses him a lot and has many

painful feelings around Duane's death.  Those feelings don't go away very fast.  Grief takes a long time.  Maybe he needs a lesson about feelings that will help him with his grief.  I better have a talk with him." Tom swam off in search of Denny and found him in a far off corner of the pond all alone.

"Hi buddy!" Tom called.  Denny didn't look up.  "Having a bad day?" Tom asked.  Denny nodded.  "I understand," said Tom.  "You do?" asked Denny as he looked up.  "Sure, there are many painful feelings when we grieve the loss of someone.  It takes a long time before the pain goes away." "It does?" asked Denny, "I thought I should be feeling better by now.  But all I can think about is Duane and I miss him so much."

"Of course you do.  We all do.  But Duane was your best friend.  You don't get over those painful feelings very quickly after someone dies, especially a good friend.  Tell me what you are feeling," said Tom.  "I don't know.  It's hard to explain.  I'm feeling all kinds of feelings," said Denny.  "That's what grief is like, we have all kinds of feelings, but it's important to get those feelings out or sometimes they will come out sideways," said Tom.  "What do you mean, sideways?" asked Denny.

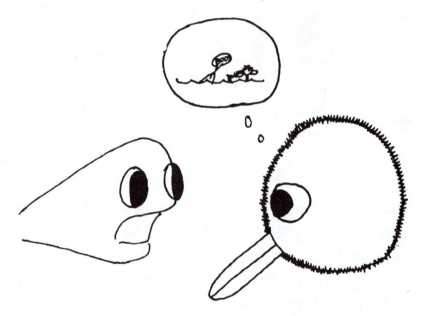

"Well, if we don't get our feelings out, sometimes we can get very angry for no reason at all," explained Tom, "Did that happen for you?"  "Yes, this morning.  Wally came up from behind me and scared me and I got mad at him.  He was just trying to make me feel better, but I yelled at him.  And now I feel bad, because I didn't mean to yell at him.

It's just that,.. It's not fair that Duane died. It's just not fair," said Duane. "You're right, it's not fair that Duane died. And I know you didn't mean to yell at Wally. It might be a good idea to go and talk to Wally and tell him how you feel. You are not mad at Wally, you're just mad that Duane died, right?" "Right," said Denny.

Tom reminded Denny that sometimes when we are feeling mad, it helps if we get lots of exercise. "Have you swam your laps today?" "No, I've been too upset," said Denny. "Well, just remember that when we are feeling upset, exercise can help us with our upset feelings."

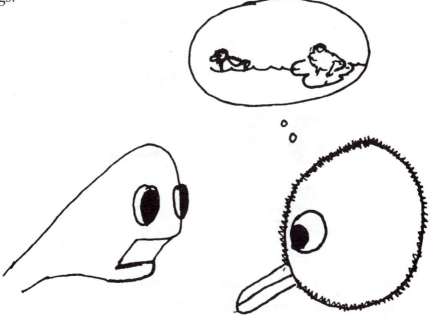

"I saw Fern the frog earlier. She said that she saw you earlier today and you swam right by," said Tom. "She said Hi?" asked Denny. "Yes, and she said that you ignored her." "No, I was just feeling so sad that I didn't want to talk to anyone," said Denny. "Well remember, it's when we are feeling so sad that we need to talk to people we can trust. You know that you can trust Fern with your feelings."

"I know," said Denny, "One more thing.  Sometimes I worry a lot and I'm scared that something else bad is going to happen.   What can I do about my scared feelings?" "Well," said Tom, "you need to learn how to relax.  I'm starting relaxation classes for everyone on the pond next week.  Maybe you would like to join.  In the meantime, you should get lots of rest, exercise a lot, eat three meals a day, and stay away from things that make you feel bad."

"You know what," said Denny, "I feel better just from talking to you." "Great!" said Tom. "Remember that there are things we can do to help us with our feelings." "I know," said Denny, "Right now I feel happy.  Thanks Tom."  Then he swam away.

## THE END

# Denny the Duck Finds Help in the Big Pond

*by Linda Lehmann*
*illustrated by John Norquist*
*edited by Shane R. Jimerson*

The days and weeks after Duane the duck died were very lonely for Denny the duck. He missed his friend and everywhere he went, he was reminded of Duane. Denny was sad every day.

Most days he just floated around in the Big Pond alone. "Duane was my best friend," thought Denny. "He was my only friend. I'll never have a friend like him. I'll never be happy again."

He passed by a rock and heard someone snoring. It was Tom the turtle taking a nap in the afternoon sun. Suddenly a leaf brushed his face and he woke up. "Oh hi," said Tom, "How are you doing Denny?" "I really miss Duane. I don't have any friends. Duane was my only friend," said Denny.

"I'll never have another friend like him," said Denny, and then he began to cry. "Well you're right about that," said Tom, "you will never have another friend like Duane. But I'll bet if you look around you, you'll find that you have lots of friends. I am your friend." "Thank you, Tom," said Denny, "That helps." Denny thought about how easy it was for him to talk to Tom about how he felt. He thought, "Everyone should have someone to tell their feelings to."

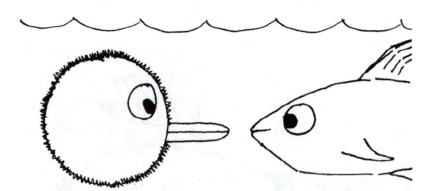

Feeling kind of hungry, he dove under water for some food. He almost bumped into Wally the walleye. "Oh!" said Denny, "Wally, you scared me! I didn't expect to find you here." "Well, where did you expect to find me? I live here," said Wally, "Fish do live in the water you know. Hey, do you want to see my new trick? Watch!" And with that Wally dove through the seaweed and hid in the mud at the bottom of the lake.

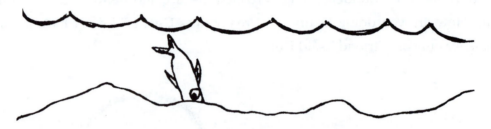

Then he came up in back of Denny and yelled, "Boo! Did I scare you?" Denny looked at Wally and started to laugh. He laughed so hard he shook all over. "What's so funny?" asked Wally. "You should see what you look like," said Denny. "You have mud and seaweed all over you. You look like some kind of monster—really ugly." "Thanks a lot!" said Wally, "Say I have not heard you laugh much since Duane died."

Denny cried all the way to shore. He got out of the water and sat down next to Duane's grave. He cried and cried. "I'm sorry Duane," he sobbed, "It's all my fault you died."

"I don't think so." He heard a voice say and he turned to see his friend Tom the turtle who was napping on a nearby rock. "Oh, you heard me crying," said Denny. "Yes," said Tom, "You have to stop blaming yourself Denny. There would have been no way for you to keep Duane from being hit by the boat. He was already in the air when you saw the boat, right?"

"We all love you and care about you, Denny. You are the most loved duck in the pond, probably in the whole world," said Fern. "Well, thank you Fern," said Denny, "I'm beginning to see that I have a lot more friends than I thought I had. You always make me feel good about me. You are a good friend to have around."

Denny swam to the shore where Duane was buried and sat by his grave. He said, "I really miss you, Duane. You were my best friend. I thought you were my only friend. But I can see I have lots of friends who want to give me help. They cannot take your place, but they are good friends. Everyone needs help from a friend sometimes. I will never forget you, Duane, but I know I have lots of help from people who care about me." Suddenly, Denny was surrounded by all of his friends and he was happy he found help in the Big Pond.

THE END

# Index

# About the Authors

**Linda Lehmann, M.A.,** is the founder and former Executive Director of the Center for Grief, Loss, and Transition in St. Paul, Minnesota. She has worked with children and adolescents for more than 30 years and has worked within the grief and loss arena since 1987. Linda Lehmann is a licensed psychologist in private practice in St. Paul and is the Bereavement Coordinator for the Children's Hospitals and Clinics in the Twin Cities.

**Shane R. Jimerson, Ph.D.,** is a professor of Developmental Studies and Counseling, Clinical, and School Psychology in the Graduate School of Education at the University of California in Santa Barbara (UCSB). Dr. Jimerson is also the Director of Project Loss at UCSB, where he studies grief and the transitions that children and families experience following a loss.

**Ann Gaasch, M.A.,** has worked with children and families since 1991, specializing in issues of bereavement, trauma, and abuse. She is a family therapist with the Harriet Tubman Family Center in Minnesota and is associated with the Center for Grief, Loss, and Transition in St. Paul, Minnesota.